THE PENGUIN CLASSICS

EDITED BY E. V. RIEU

GIOVANNI DELLA CASA

# GALATEO

OR

## THE BOOK OF MANNERS

*A new translation by*
R. S. PINE-COFFIN

PENGUIN BOOKS

Penguin Books Ltd, Harmondsworth, Middlesex
U.S.A.: Penguin Books Inc., 3300 Clipper Mill Road, Baltimore 11, Md
AUSTRALIA: Penguin Books Pty Ltd, 762 Whitehorse Road,
Mitcham, Victoria

—

This translation first published 1958

—

The roundel on the jacket shows the
arms of the Della Casa family taken from
Ughello's *Italia Sacra*, 1721

Made and printed in Great Britain
by Unwin Brothers Ltd,
Woking and London

# Contents

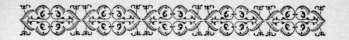

## Introduction

AMONG the world's books on social behaviour the *Galateo* holds a unique position. Although it was written almost exactly four hundred years ago, so far from suffering the fate of most books of courtesy, it has survived the successive changes in the morals and manners of society and its maxims are as true today as when they were first written. The name *Galateo*, in fact, has become proverbial in Italy, where it is said of anyone whose manners are not all they should be that 'he does not know his *Galateo*' – *non conosce il Galateo* – and a polite reprimand about his behaviour may be introduced by saying *Monsignor Della Casa dice* – 'Monsignor Della Casa says'. This is not to say that all who so glibly make use of the author's name have themselves read his book or are even aware of who he was. But proverbs are not lightly coined, and the fact remains that most educated Italians are familiar with the work which gave rise to this one. It has remained constantly in print throughout four centuries and a choice of several editions is available in Italian bookshops today.

Etiquette is as fickle as fashion. It varies from age to age, from country to country, and even from class to class. The *Galateo* does not deal with such quicksilver as this, but with something far more fundamental. For example, courtesy demands that a man should greet his friends when he meets them. If he does not, they will take it as a snub, a rebuke, or a demonstration of indifference. But whether he greets them by shaking hands, raising his hat, bowing, or even rubbing noses, is a matter for etiquette. The *Galateo* is not so much concerned with these niceties as with the foundations of good behaviour, which are the same for all nations and all classes. For etiquette is merely a system of conventions, by which the principles of good manners are applied.

The principle on which the *Galateo* is based is that no man should do anything to offend or displease another. This is nothing new, and it was not new in the sixteenth century, for it is simply a re-statement of the Christian duty of charity. But this was not the angle from which Della Casa chose to approach the question. Nor did he make any appeal to sentiment or emotion. Manners, for him, are a matter of expediency and 'do as you would be done by', and though he tells us that good manners come near to virtue, he does not base his argument on moral issues. He condemns vice, not because it is sinful, but because, being evil, it is ugly and consequently offensive. And offence can be given in more innocuous ways as well; through the physical senses of taste, smell, and so on; through the imagination, by reminding others of unpleasant things; or by thwarting their intentions or grating upon the natural sense of what is right and fitting in an orderly world. Plenty of examples are given, some of them amusing, so that the reader may be forewarned and avoid displeasing others through mere thoughtlessness. When he has learnt this lesson, he must attempt the more positive task of acquiring grace and charm. He will then be welcome wherever he goes, and as well as giving pleasure to others by his company he will be able to enjoy all the benefits that friendship can provide.

It must not be supposed from this scanty analysis that the *Galateo* is a dry tract intended for moralists and philosophers. It is true that Alfieri was disgusted by the portentous word *conciosiacosaché* with which the first chapter begins and, according to his own account,[1] threw his copy out of the window in a fit of rage. Nevertheless, later on, he read it many times over, for in spite of its alarming overture the book is addressed to a young man of the world, generally supposed to be Della Casa's nephew, Annibale Rucellai. It is written in a benign and friendly

1. Vittorio Alfieri, *Vita scritta da esso*, epoca 4, cap. 1.

style and, to avoid giving it an air of pedantry, the author pretends to be quite unlearned and unlettered. It might seem from the numerous references to Boccaccio that he sometimes forgets his part, but it must be remembered that anyone who could read was certain to be familiar with the *Decameron*.

The title *Galateo* may puzzle English readers. It is derived from the name of Galeazzo (Galateus) Florimonte, Bishop of Aquino and later of Sesso, whom Della Casa met in Rome in 1543. He was widely famous as a model of intellectual and moral probity at a time when laxity in these matters was fairly general. Because of these qualities he was chosen to serve at the Council of Trent during the period of its first sessions at Trent and Bologna. He again met Della Casa in Rome about 1550 and suggested to him the idea of writing a book to guide the ordinary man in the principles of civilized living, a subject which, as we shall see later, was very much in vogue. This was how the *Galateo* acquired its title. Florimonte is mentioned in chapter 4 in an anecdote about the court of Bishop Giberti at Verona, where he resided from 1533 to 1536.

Giovanni Della Casa was born in 1503 of a family of wealthy landowners, probably at La Casa del Mugello near Florence, though his exact birthplace is not known. Soon afterwards his father left Florence for Bologna, taking his family with him, and it was here that the young Giovanni had his first schooling. As a young man he studied law in Florence and later at Padua, where he first met Pietro Bembo, who was to become a great friend to him later in life. About 1530 he settled in Florence, intending to obtain a post in the government service, but he soon relinquished this plan in favour of residing in Rome, where he went about 1534.

Although he took minor orders about this time – the precise date is not known – he apparently had no intention at this stage of proceeding to the priesthood. As was the custom at the time, he purchased for himself the title of *chierico della Camera Apostolica* and secured nominal employment in the papal government. However, his official duties did not occupy him greatly and he seems to have divided his time between study and dissolute living. During this period he wrote his first verses, some of which he himself later described as *non castissimi*, and an elegant Latin essay, called *Quaestio lepidissima an uxor sit ducenda*, which is now generally acknowledged as his work, though in the past there was some doubt as to its authenticity. His compositions soon attracted the attention of prominent members of Roman society and won him the patronage of Pope Paul III and his nephew, Cardinal Alessandro Farnese, who remained his lifelong friend.

In 1541 he was sent to Florence as commissioner for the Pope's tithes and had the honour of being accepted into the Accademia Fiorentina, previously known as Accademia degli Umidi, which during its long history had numbered many important literary figures among its members. Three years later, in 1544, he was elected Archbishop of Benevento and was ordained priest in order to qualify for this office, but he never visited his diocese, for in the same year he was appointed Papal Nuncio to the republic of Venice. Before leaving Rome to take up his appointment he handed over his house and his vineyards near the Porta del Popolo to the care of Pietro Bembo, who described him as '*tanto amico mio, quanto niuno altro uomo, che io in Roma abbia*' – 'the greatest friend I have in Rome'.

The period of his nunciature in Venice was the climax of his ecclesiastical and political career. As the Pope's representative it was his duty to steer the Inquisition on a safe course, a delicate task in a city where Lutheranism was gaining a foothold and the government refused to co-operate. It fell to his lot to indict Pier Paolo Vergerio, Bishop of Capo d'Istria, for heresy, and this was the occasion of one of his finest Latin works, the *Dissertatio adversus Paulum Vergerium*. Vergerio was deprived of his see and took refuge in Switzerland, where he openly professed Lutheran doctrines and published a malicious attack on Della Casa, accusing him of writing obscene verses and reviling him for the list of prohibited books which he had drawn up in 1548.

Although he was persistently troubled with gout and was much occupied with official business, Della Casa still found time to write poems in both Latin and Italian. His political writings, the *Orazione per la Lega* and the *Orazione scritta a Carlo V Imperadore intorno alla restituzione della città di Piacenza* also date from this period. In 1550, his nunciature over, he returned to Rome, perhaps in the hope of being rewarded for his services with a cardinal's hat. But Paul III had died in 1549 and his other protector, Cardinal Alessandro Farnese, was away from Rome. He left again for Venice in 1551, happy enough to live in retirement. Part of his time was spent in the city and part in the country near Treviso where, besides further poems, he wrote the *Galateo* and, in Latin, the lives of Pietro Bembo and Cardinal Gaspare Contarini, the Catholic reformer.

In 1555 the new Pope, Paul IV, was persuaded by Alessandro Farnese to invite Della Casa to come to Rome as secretary of state. At first he was unwilling to accept the office, but the invitation was turned into a command which he could not refuse. It was generally expected that he would now receive his cardinal's hat, but when his name was not among those of the newly created cardinals in December 1555, many supposed that his lack of preferment was due to the salacious tone of his early verses, lately given prominence in Vergerio's pamphlet. It is more probable that Paul IV was anxious to show no partiality, and it was Della Casa's misfortune to have been recommended by Henry II of France, to whom he was distantly related by marriage through Queen Catherine de' Medici. He died in November 1556 after an illness of some months and was buried in the church of S. Andrea della Valle in Rome.

Besides the works already mentioned Della Casa left letters in Latin and Italian; a speech *Delle lodi della*

*Serenissima Repubblica di Venezia*, which he delivered before the nobility of Venice; a short treatise *De officiis inter potentiores et tenuiores amicos*, which is generally considered as a continuation of the *Galateo* and which he himself translated into Italian; Latin translations of some of the speeches from Thucydides; and a political brief drawn up on behalf of Paul IV, entitled *Istruzione al Cardinale Caraffa sopra il negozio della pace tra Enrico II, Re di Francia, e Filippo II, Re di Spagna*.

The *Galateo*, which was his major work, was written between 1551 and 1555. It was first published posthumously in Venice in 1558 in a volume which also contained the *Rime* and the *Orazione scritta a Carlo V*. A year later it was printed again in Milan, this time on its own. It was translated into French in 1562, Latin in 1580, Spanish in 1585, and German in 1597. The first English version was the work of Robert Peterson, of Lincoln's Inn, and was published in 1576 with a dedication to Robert Dudley, Earl of Leicester. The translation was most probably made from an anonymous French version of 1573, and though it is reasonably accurate, its archaic language is tiresome to the modern reader unless he is fond of quaint phraseology. There followed in 1701 a new version made 'by several young gentlemen educated at a private grammar school near Hackney'. A third edition by an anonymous translator, based with considerable freedom on the Latin version of Nathan Chytraeus, appeared in 1703, and a fourth by the poet and novelist Richard Graves was published in 1774. Graves, who used the Italian text and took obvious liberties with it, rightly called his work a paraphrase rather than a translation. Besides these editions an epitomized version was included in *The Rich Cabinet*, an anonymous book on social behaviour published in 1616, and an inaccurate paraphrase by Nathaniel Waker, entitled *The Refined Courtier*, with interpolations by the translator, went into print in 1663.

Books of manners, except for the sort which legislate

upon the etiquette of eating peas or folding table napkins, are nowadays out of fashion. But when the *Galateo* was written the modern world was still young and the manners of the dark ages had not yet disappeared, if indeed they have entirely disappeared even today. It was commonly agreed that Italy led the world, not only in the new learning, but also in the arts and all the polite accomplishments of civilization. Young men from England and the rest of Europe flocked to her universities to study and equip themselves with the art of courteous living, just as they were later to wander over the Continent on the Grand Tour. At the same time more and more books translated from the Italian were reaching the English bookstalls, 'fonde books' as Roger Ascham called them, 'sold in every shop in London, commended by the honest titles the sooner to corrupt honest manners'. We may not all agree with Ascham, but it was not surprising that the Italianate Englishman at home became a familiar figure of fun, for not all of those who read these books or went abroad to learn their manners also learned discretion. There were many in England who listened to the

> Report of fashions in proud Italy,
> Whose manners still our tardy apish nation
> Limps after in base imitation.[1]

This was the public which Peterson hoped to serve when he translated the *Galateo*. It was by no means the first book on social duties to reach the English reader, for Caxton had printed at Westminster in 1487 his own translation of Jacques Le Grand's *Book of Good Manners*, and Alexander Barclay's *Mirror of Good Manners*, translated from Domenico Mancini's *De quatuor virtutibus*, had been published in 1523. Both of these books – and there were others like them – contained practical maxims for daily life; but 'manners' meant the practice of the moral code and a standard of conduct based on humility, patience,

1. Shakespeare, *Richard II*, II, i, 21–23.

justice, temperance, and the other Christian virtues. More suited to the temperament of the new era was Baldassare Castiglione's *Cortegiano* and this, very properly translated by Sir Thomas Hoby, himself a courtier and diplomat who had studied at Padua, was published in English in 1561.

The *Cortegiano* presents us with an exceptionally clear picture of the ideal gentleman of the Renaissance. Besides the traditional qualities of chivalry and courage, he was now expected to be a wise counsellor, a lover of the arts, and something of a scholar. He was to be 'well borne and of a good stocke', 'well spoken and faire languaged', 'wise and well seene in discourses upon states' and 'more than indifferentlye well seene in learninge, in the Latin and Greeke tungues' (Hoby's analysis). He also had to know how 'to play upon the lute, and singe to it with the ditty' as well as 'to be skilfull in all kynd of marciall feates'. He was to make himself an expert at fencing, tennis, hunting, hawking, riding, swimming, wrestling, jousting, and other sports, though he was to be careful not to 'renn, wrastle, leape nor cast the stone or barr with men of the countrey, except he be sure to gete the victorie'.

All this is set forth in four books which describe the perfect qualities of a courtier and a 'waytinge gentil-woman', even instructing them how to make use of 'merie jestes and pranckes'. Roger Ascham, a notorious opponent of everything Italian, welcomed the appearance of Hoby's translation and recommended it as suitable reading for the young. This was six years before Peterson published his version of the *Galateo*, but it is not unlikely that Ascham would have found in the new book yet another exception to his rule.

The *Cortegiano* was intended for rather exalted circles – 'yonge gentilmen and gentilwomen abiding in court, palaice, or place'. With the *Galateo*, dealing as it does with the minor diplomacy of everyday human relationships, Della Casa aimed to serve a wider public, perhaps what we should call the 'middle class', but certainly not the 'lower class'. For though the book is intended for ordinary people, it is quite plain that the author thought some people more ordinary than others. The youth to whom it is addressed comes of a respectable family and is not allowed to forget it. He is told, for instance, not to run in the street in case he pants or sweats, but there is no reason why his groom should not exert himself in this way, since, presumably, perspiration is less unbecoming in a groom. But, for all this, it is obvious that far more people can aspire to the ideals of the *Galateo* than to those of the *Cortegiano*, and this is why, of the two, the *Galateo* has suffered less from the passage of time. In more than one place it is clearly reminiscent of the earlier work, but literary piracy was common and Della Casa at least had the courtesy to acknowledge that there had been *migliori dettatori e maestri* before him.

This is the background against which the *Galateo* should be read. But the picture of Italian books of courtesy would not be complete without some mention of Stefano Guazzo's *La civil conversatione*, translated into English by George Pettie and Bartholomew Young in 1581. This book is now forgotten, but with the *Cortegiano* and the *Galateo* it formed a trio of textbooks which long remained in favour. The three books are recommended in *The Voyage of Italy*, a book written in 1670 by Richard Lassels, a professional escort of young gentlemen travelling on the Grand Tour. Perhaps the passage against which the titles appear as marginal references is worth quoting. 'As for their [i.e. the Italians'] manners, they are most commendable. They have taught them in their books, they practise them in their actions, and they have spread them abroad over all Europe, which owes its civility unto the Italians, as well as its religion.'

The best modern edition of the *Galateo* is that of Giovanni Tinivella (fourth revised printing, Milan, 1954), which I have largely used for this translation and to which I am indebted for its helpful introduction. I have also used

Giovanni Battista Casotti's edition of the complete works of Della Casa (Florence, 1707), which contains a long, though somewhat rambling and not entirely reliable account of the author's life and works. As far as I am aware, there are no books in English on Della Casa.

R. S. P-C.

# THE TREATISE OF
# GIOVANNI DELLA CASA

## CALLED

# GALATEO

## OR THE BOOK OF MANNERS

*in which the author
assumes the character of an old man without
pretence of learning and instructs
a young pupil on what to do and what
not to do in the general
company of friends*

## CHAPTER I

*Preamble – Scope of the discussion – Good manners
compared with other more heroic virtues – Usefulness
of the lessons we are to learn and the ease with which
they may be put into practice*

IN as much as you are now at the start of life's
journey, which I have, as you can see, for the most
part completed, the great affection which I have for
you leads me to come forward and point out some of
the places in your path where, as experience has taught
me, I fear you may easily stumble or be led astray. I
hope that under my guidance you may follow a
straight course, to the salvation of your soul and the
honour and glory of your noble and distinguished
family.

Since instruction on matters of more substance or
greater subtlety is likely to be beyond the grasp of
one of your tender age, I will reserve these things for
a more suitable time and begin with something which
many people might well think trivial; that is to say,
how, in my opinion, we should behave if we wish to
be courteous, agreeable, and good-mannered in our
conversation and dealings with others. If this is not
virtue, it is not far removed from it. For though
generosity, loyalty, and moral courage are without
doubt nobler and more praiseworthy qualities than
charm and courtesy, nevertheless polite habits and a
correct manner of speech and behaviour may benefit
those who possess them no less than a noble spirit

and a stout heart benefit others. For since each one of us is daily obliged to meet other people and converse with them, we need to use our manners many times each day. But justice, fortitude, and the other virtues of the higher and nobler sort are needed less frequently. We are not required to practise generosity or mercy at all hours, nor could any man do so very often. Similarly, those who are endowed with courage and strength are seldom called upon to show their valour by their deeds.

Although such qualities are of a higher order and carry greater weight, the points of good behaviour are more numerous and more frequently practised. If it served any purpose, I could give you the names of many men, both living and dead, who have won much favour solely by reason of their charm and elegance, though in other respects they were of little account. Thanks to this advantage they reached the very highest positions, far outstripping others who were gifted with the finer and more admirable qualities which we have mentioned. Polite and agreeable manners can win for us the goodwill of those with whom we live, just as clumsy, uncouth behaviour leads them to hate and despise us.

For that matter, although the law prescribes no penalty for rudeness and bad manners, treating them as slight offences – for, of course, they are not grave crimes – nevertheless we can see that nature herself punishes us for them severely by depriving us on their account of the friendship and company of others. Serious crimes do more harm, but these lesser offences cause more nuisance or, at least, cause it more often. Men are frightened of wild beasts, but they have no fear of some of the small animals, such as mosquitoes and flies, which, nevertheless, by continual irritation, trouble them more often than the others. In the same way most of us dislike rude, disagreeable people as much as criminals, and perhaps more so.

For this reason no one need doubt that a person who proposes to live in a civilized place among other men, rather than in a desert or a hermitage, will find it most useful to know how to behave with courtesy and tact. Furthermore, other forms of virtue need greater resources and they are of little or no avail without them. But manners are rich and powerful in themselves, although they are made up of nothing more than words and actions.

CHAPTER 2

*Bad manners analysed –*
*Definition of obnoxious behaviour according*
*to the senses which it offends*

To help you understand how to behave I must first teach you that your conduct should not be governed by your own fancy, but in consideration of the feelings of those whose company you keep. This must be done with discretion, because a man who is too ready to defer to others in conversation and etiquette appears not so much a gentleman as a fool or a joker or even a flatterer. On the other hand, a person who does not trouble to consider the likes and dislikes of other people is coarse, rude, and unfriendly.

Therefore, since good manners depend upon consideration of other people's wishes instead of our own pleasure, if we can establish which things most people like, and which they dislike, we shall easily discover what to do and what to avoid in their company.

Let us conclude, then, that the unpleasant things which we should not do are those which offend any of the senses or cause disgust, as well as anything that reminds others of matters distasteful to them or painful to think about.

## CHAPTER 3

*Some of the things which offend the senses and are therefore unpleasant, and sometimes disgusting, even to think of*

SINCE indelicate or immodest actions, or those which cause disgust and turn the stomach, should not be performed in the presence of others, it follows that one should also refrain from mentioning them. And not only should they not be performed or discussed, but any behaviour suggestive of them is very distressing to others.

For this reason it is a repulsive habit to touch certain parts of the body in public, as some people do. Similarly, no polite person will prepare himself for the relief of nature while others are looking on. Nor, when he has done, will he readjust his clothes in their presence. I would also advise him, when he returns from these duties, not to wash his hands in the sight of respectable company, because the reason for which he is washing has ugly implications.

For the same reason it is bad manners, when you see something to nauseate you by the roadside, as sometimes happens, to turn to your companions and point it out to them. Still less should you offer any evil smelling object for others to sniff, as some people do, insisting upon holding it up to their noses and asking them to smell how horrible it is. Far better warn them not to smell it.

Just as this sort of behaviour is offensive to the sense of smell, you should also refrain as far as possible from making noises which grate upon the ear, such as grinding or sucking your teeth, making things squeak, or allowing rough stones or metal objects to scrape together and rasp. Moreover, you should take care not to sing, especially solo, if your voice is discordant and tuneless. Many people are thoughtless about this and, in fact, the most frequent offenders seem to be those who have the least gift for singing.

Some others, with their coughing and sneezing, make enough din to deafen everyone else or use so little restraint that they spray the faces of those who are near them. There are also people who howl or bray like asses when they yawn, and some try to continue talking with their mouths still open, so that their voices sound like the noises a dumb man makes in the effort to speak. You should beware of this, because it is tiresome both to hear and to see.

There is another reason, too, why polite persons should try to control their yawning, because if they do it too often, they appear bored or depressed, as though they found the company and their conversation and ways tedious and would prefer to be elsewhere. Moreover, though we are quite ready to yawn at any time, it will not occur to us to do so if we are busy and our thoughts are occupied. But when we are idle and have nothing to do, the inducement to yawn is great. This is why a group of people taking their leisure together unconcernedly will irresistibly follow suit, as you must often have noticed, if one of their number yawns, as though he had reminded them of something which they would have done before if they had thought of it. I have often heard learned men say that in Latin the same word is used for yawning as for being idle and unoccupied. So we ought to avoid this habit which, as I have said, is unpleasant to hear, to see, and to think of, because it not only shows that the company we are with is little to our liking, but also reveals our own drowsiness and stupefaction; and this is a failing which will not endear us to our companions.

Again, when you have blown your nose, you should not open your handkerchief and inspect it, as though pearls or rubies had dropped out of your skull. Such behaviour is nauseating and is more likely to lose us the affection of those who love us than to win us the favour of others. This is proved in the *Corbaccio*, where the spirit, whoever he may have been, in order to cure Boccaccio of his passion for a woman of whom he knew little, told him that she squatted over a brazier coughing and spitting up rheum.

It is also an unpleasant habit to lift another person's glass of wine or his food to your nose and smell it. I would even advise you not to smell your own food and drink, because drops may fall from your nose, and even the thought that this may happen is disgusting. I must also recommend you not to offer anyone else a glass of wine which you have tasted and touched with your lips, unless he is a very close intimate of yours. Still less should you offer him a pear or any other fruit from which you have already taken a bite. Do not imagine that these things are unimportant. For even gentle blows can kill if they are plentiful enough.

## CHAPTER 4

*To prove that details must not be overlooked,*
*there follows an account of what Galateo did to Count*
*Ricciardo at the behest of the Bishop of Verona*

THERE was once in Verona a very wise and learned
bishop named Giovanni Matteo Giberti. Amongst
his other virtues he used to treat all the distinguished
persons who visited him with great courtesy and hos-
pitality, entertaining them with all the honours in his
house, not extravagantly but with moderation, as
befits one in Holy Orders. At the time of which I am
speaking it so happened that a nobleman named Count
Ricciardo came to Verona and stayed for several days
with the bishop and his household, most of whom
were persons of culture and learning. They found
much to commend and admire in the count's gentle
breeding and fine manners, except that he had one
small fault. The bishop, who was a very discerning
man, noticed this failing and called some of his
closest friends together to discuss how they might best
bring it to the count's attention without giving him
offence. Accordingly, when the count had taken his
leave and was due to depart the next morning, the
bishop sent for one of his friends, whose discretion
he trusted, and instructed him to ride out and accom-
pany the count for part of the way. As soon as he
thought fit he was to find means to tell the count tactfully about the matter which they had discussed.
The bishop's friend was an old man of great learning,
gifted with indescribable charm in speech and
demeanour, who in his time had much frequented
the courts of the nobility. His name was Galateo and,
for all I know, if he is alive, he is still known by that

name. It was at his request and on his advice that I set out to write this book.

As he rode along with the count, he soon engaged him in pleasant conversation, leading from one subject to another, until the time came for him to turn back to Verona. He begged leave of the count and wished him godspeed, saying with a friendly smile, 'Sir, my lord the bishop is exceedingly grateful for the honour you have done him by coming to his humble house and staying with him. He has also asked me to make you a gift on his behalf, in recognition of the great courtesy you have shown him. He earnestly begs you to accept it in good heart, and this is what I have to impart to you.

'In the bishop's opinion, he has met no man more courteous and mannerly than yourself, and therefore he has studied your behaviour closely and examined it in every particular. He has found that it is in all points most engaging and commendable except for this one shortcoming, that when you are eating at table you make a strange noise with your mouth and lips, which is very distressing to hear. The bishop has asked me to draw your attention to it and begs that you should do your utmost to guard against it. In place of a parting gift he prays you to accept this friendly reproof and admonition, for he is certain that no one else in the world would bestow it upon you.'

The count, who until then had been unconscious of his failing, blushed slightly to hear himself admonished for it. But, like the good man he was, he soon recovered himself and replied, 'Please tell the bishop that men would be far richer than they are, if all the gifts which they exchange were the equal of his. Return him my unbounded thanks for his great affability and kindness towards me, and assure him that for the future I shall most certainly take the greatest pains to correct this fault. May God be with you!'

## CHAPTER 5

*Continuing the discussion of the bad habits which are offensive to the senses*

WHAT, then, might we expect the bishop and his honourable friends to say to those people whom we sometimes see with their snouts buried greedily in their plates, like pigs, never raising their faces or lifting their eyes, still less their hands, from the food? They eat, or rather, gobble with both cheeks bloated as though they were sounding a trumpet or blowing the fire, and by smearing their hands and arms with food almost to the elbow they soil their napkins until they are dirtier than slop-cloths. Very often they are not even ashamed to use the same napkins to wipe away the sweat which haste and over-eating bring out in drops on their foreheads, on their faces, and around their necks. They will even use them to blow their noses if they feel like it. Of course persons of this sort would not deserve to be admitted to the noble bishop's punctilious household. In fact, they should be entirely excluded from any place where respectable people are to be found. A man who knows how to behave will take care not to get his fingers so greasy as to dirty his napkin with them, because the sight of it would be unsavoury to others. Nor is it polite to wipe them on the bread which he is going to eat.

The upper servants, who wait at table, must in no circumstances scratch their heads or other parts of the body in front of their master when he is at dinner, nor should they touch any of the parts of the body which are normally covered. They should not even look as if they were touching them, as some careless servants do when they tuck their hands in the top of their aprons or clasp them behind their backs under their coat-tails. They must hold them where they can be seen, so that no one need be apprehensive, and they must keep them washed and scrupulously clean without the least trace of dirtiness about them.

Those who serve the dishes or pour the wine must take care not to spit or cough, and still more not to sneeze, while they are performing these duties. It is just as objectionable for the diners to suspect the waiters of such conduct as actually to witness it, and since a supposed misdemeanour is as aggravating as a real one, servants should be on their guard not to give their masters cause for suspicion. If you ever have to roast a pear before the fire or toast bread in the embers, do not try to blow away any ashes which may adhere to them. Instead, remember the saying that there is never wind without rain, and shake off the ashes by gently tapping the dish or by some other method. Never offer your handkerchief to anyone, however clean it may be, because the other person does not know whether it is clean and might find it repulsive.

When you are talking to someone, you should not approach him so close as to breathe in his face. You will learn that many people dislike the sensation of another's breath, even if it is not tainted.

Objectionable behaviour of this sort must be avoided because, as I said before, it may be offensive to one or other of the five senses. Now let us consider the kind of conduct which causes displeasure, not because it is offensive to the senses, but because it conflicts with the wishes of the majority of the company.

## CHAPTER 6

*An explanation of the pleasures which people derive from each other's company, followed by a discussion of the ways in which their enjoyment may be spoilt – Indiscretions which betray lack of interest in the conversation*

You must understand that men's natural desires are many and various. Some seek to vent their anger, others to satisfy their greed, their lust, their covetousness, or various other passions. But these are not the purposes they have in mind or expect to attain simply by consorting together, for such things have nothing to do with conventional behaviour and polite conversation. It must be, then, that they look for something which they can obtain from each other's company, and this can only be kindness, esteem, recreation, or other pleasures of the same kind. This being so, they should neither say nor do anything to show dislike or disparagement of the other persons present.

This is why it is unmannerly to fall asleep, as many people do, whilst the company is engaged in conversation. Their conduct shows that they have little respect for their friends and care nothing either for them or their talk. Besides, they are generally obliged to doze in an uncomfortable position, and this nearly always causes them to make unpleasant noises and gestures in their sleep. Often enough they begin to sweat and dribble at the mouth.

For the same reason it is irritating to stand up and walk about the room whilst the others remain seated and continue their conversation. Some people, too, will fidget and writhe, stretch themselves and yawn, turning from one side to the other, as if the fever were upon them, and making it obvious that they find the company dull.

Just as bad as these people are those who continually take letters from their pockets and read them. Even worse are those who bring out their scissors and set about cutting their nails. It shows that they have little interest in their companions and are trying to find some other amusement to pass the time.

Neither should you adopt the habit, which some people have, of humming to yourself, drumming with your fingers, or swinging your legs. Such behaviour shows your indifference towards other people. Likewise, no one should place himself in such a position as to turn his back on anyone else, nor raise either of his legs so as to expose those parts of the body which are usually concealed. These things are done only in the presence of people who need not be treated with deference. In fact, if a gentleman were to behave in this way before a member of his household or even a friend of lesser degree than himself, it would be a sign of friendship and familiarity rather than arrogance.

Everyone should stand erect, without leaning on other people or bending over them. Many people will interrupt another when he is speaking, nudging him with their elbows at every word and saying, 'What did I tell you?', 'What do you say to that?', or 'How about so and so?'

## CHAPTER 7

### *How to dress without disrespect to others*

EVERYONE should dress well, according to his age and his position in society. If he does not, it will be taken as a mark of contempt for other people. This is why the citizens of Padua used to consider themselves slighted when the fine gentlemen of Venice visited their city wearing heavy coats, as though they thought they were in the country. Not only should a man's clothes be made of fine cloth, but he should also do his best to follow the prevailing fashion and conform with local customs, even though he may find, or think he finds, them less comfortable and becoming than the ones he is used to. If everyone in town has short hair, it is wrong to grow long tresses, just as it is wrong to go clean-shaven if everyone else has a beard, because this implies contradiction of others, which is a thing never to be done except in case of necessity, as we shall see later on. In fact, more than anything else it will make others dislike us.

In this matter, then, you should not set yourself against accepted customs but should discreetly observe them. In this way you will not be the only one to wear a long-tailed coat reaching to your ankles where everyone else wears a short, waist-length one. For just as everybody turns to stare at a man whose face is ugly – which is another way of saying that it is different from the normal fashion of nature – so it is with persons who dress to suit themselves, quite differently from everyone else, growing their hair in a long mane, trimming their beards or shaving them off, or wearing skull-caps or those big, German-style hats. Everyone turns to gape at them, pressing around them as they do with people who are ready to challenge all comers.

Clothes should also fit well and suit the wearer. People who have fine and elegant garments, but wear them so untidily that they look as if they were made for someone else, show either that they are indifferent whether they please other people or not, or that they lack taste and discrimination. Their manner of dress leads the people with whom they associate to suppose that they have no respect for them, and for this reason they are unwelcome and unpopular in most circles.

## CHAPTER 8

*On people who always upset the rest of the company*
*– Perversity and petulance – The odiousness of pride*
*and the need to beware of anything which savours of it*

SOME people do more than simply draw suspicion upon themselves. By their behaviour they make it absolutely impossible for others to put up with them, because they always keep everybody waiting and cause inconvenience and discomfort. They are always unpunctual and disorderly and never find things to their liking. When the dinner is ready and everyone else has washed his hands and is about to sit down at table, these people ask for paper to write on, or demand to go to the lavatory, or remember that they have not taken their constitutional. 'It is still early,' they say. 'Surely you can wait a little. Why is there so much hurry this morning?' They are a nuisance to everybody, thinking only of themselves and their own comfort, without a shadow of consideration for others. Besides this, they always want to get the best of everything for themselves. They must sleep in the best beds in the best rooms. They must take the most comfortable chairs and sit in the place of honour. They must be served and made comfortable before others. Nothing pleases them except what they have arranged themselves, and they turn up their noses at everything else. They expect others to wait for them to take their meals, to go out riding, or to take their recreations and their pleasures.

There are other people again who are so cross-grained, perverse, and petulant that nothing will satisfy them. Whatever is said to them they always answer with a wry face. They are never done with scolding and finding fault with their servants and they continually make difficulties for everyone. 'What a fine time you called me this morning!' they complain. 'Look how well you have cleaned this shoe! And you did not even attend me to church. You wretch, I have half a mind to slap your face.'

This disgraceful rudeness must be avoided like the plague. For, however humble a man may be at heart, if he behaves in this way, even though not with malice but impulsively or from habit, he will, nevertheless, incur the hatred of other people, because outwardly his behaviour seems to spring from pride. To be proud is simply to treat others with contempt and, as we have seen, everyone likes to be respected even though he does not deserve it.

Not long ago there was in Rome a distinguished man named Ubaldino Bandinelli, who was gifted with great acumen and profound learning. He used to say that of all the noble courtiers, prelates, and lords, and of all the poor and the persons of mean and low degree whom he met in the streets as he went to the

Pope's palace or came from it, not one seemed either better or worse than himself. Of course few of them can have been his equals in merit, for his own excellence was unbounded. But qualities of this sort cannot be measured by a special yardstick. A man's worth must be appraised generously, as a miller weighs grain, not by the pennyweight on the goldsmith's scales. He should be accepted as we accept a coin, not for its intrinsic worth, but at its face-value. Therefore, when we are with people whom we wish to please, our behaviour should be friendly rather than patronizing. In fact everything that we do should in some way show our consideration and respect for our companions.

For this reason there are some things which we cannot do without disrespect for the company we are with and the place we are in, although it is not wrong to do them at the proper time. For example, as we said before, it is wrong to abuse our servants and scold them in public, and still worse to strike them, because this is a demonstration of authority and prerogative which no one should exercise in the presence of those whom he respects. If he does he will shock everyone else and spoil their enjoyment, and it will be worse still if he does it at table, which is the place for cheerfulness and not for shocks. This is why Currado Gianfigliazzi politely refrained from disconcerting his guests by taking Chichibio to task, although he richly deserved to be punished for having chosen to offend his master rather than Brunetta. It would have done Currado more credit if he had made even less fuss than he did, for he did wrong to invoke God's help to uphold his threats.[1]

1. This refers to the fourth tale of the sixth day of Boccaccio's *Decameron*. Gianfigliazzi's cook, Chichibio, cut off the leg of a crane

But, to get back to our discussion, I repeat that no one should lose his temper at table, no matter what happens. If he gets angry, he should not let it be seen nor should he give any sign of his displeasure, for the reasons I have already given, especially if guests are present. The guests were invited to enjoy themselves, but if the host is ill-tempered they will be dejected. For it is distressing to see another man suffer, just as it sets our own teeth on edge to see anyone else eating food which tastes bitter.

## CHAPTER 9

*How perverseness can part friends – The need to show others that we love them and value their love*

PERVERSENESS means wanting to have everything different from other people. The word itself shows this, for 'perverse' simply means 'the wrong way round'. You may easily imagine just how effective perverseness is likely to be in winning friends, since it consists in opposing the wishes of other people. This is to be expected of an enemy, but is not usual amongst friends. Anyone who wants to be liked should therefore guard against this fault, because it breeds hatred and chagrin instead of gratification and goodwill. In fact it is advisable to make the other person's wishes your own pleasure, unless suffering

---

which he was cooking for his master and gave it to his mistress, Brunetta. When the remainder of the bird was served at table, Gianfigliazzi asked why one of its legs was missing. Chichibio replied that cranes had only one leg. Gianfigliazzi, therefore, rather than remonstrate with his servant in the presence of his guests, told him to show him by next day a live crane with only one leg, swearing that he would be punished if he did not do so.

or disgrace will result, and let your words and actions suit his inclinations rather than your own.

You should not be uncouth or awkward but affable and friendly, for the difference between the myrtle and the butcher's broom is that one is a cultivated plant and the other grows wild.

The persons whom we like are the kind who behave in all circumstances as friends behave amongst themselves. Surly people seem like strangers everywhere – you might even say like intruders – whereas amiable people on the other hand seem to have friends and acquaintances wherever they go. We ought therefore to make a habit of greeting each other and speaking and replying to others kindly and treating everyone as friends and neighbours. Some people do not understand this. They never have a kind look for anyone; they are always ready to say no to any proposal; like eccentrics and savages, they never accept in good part any kindness or honour which may be done to them; they cannot abide visitors or companions; they find no pleasure in quips and pleasantries and refuse all offers made to them. If you say 'So and so has asked me to convey his regards to you', they will reply 'What do I care for his regards?' Or you say 'So and so asked me how you were'. 'Then let him come and feel my pulse' is the answer you get. Little wonder that such people have few friends.

It is also impolite to be gloomy or meditative in your own home. This may perhaps be permissible in those who spend much time in the contemplation of what, so I am told, are called the liberal arts, but it certainly cannot be tolerated in anyone else. In fact even those who contemplate the arts would do well to withdraw from the company of others when they wish to do their thinking.

## CHAPTER 10

*More about the pleasures we look for in conversation
and the things which may spoil them, particularly
faddiness and susceptibility*

FASTIDIOUSNESS and sensitiveness are most undesirable, especially in men. Dealing with people of this sort is more like servitude than companionship. Some of them are so dainty and easily upset that living with them is much like settling down amongst so many panes of thin glass. They are frightened of the slightest blow and must be treated and cared for accordingly. If you are not quick and attentive in greeting them, visiting them, paying them your respects, and replying to their remarks, they are just as offended by this as anyone else would be by a mortal insult. Unless you are scrupulous in giving them their proper titles, the most bitter complaints and deadly antagonisms will at once result.

'You called me by my surname without saying "Mister". Why was that? Do I not call you "Mister"? And you did not give me my proper place at table. Nor did you trouble to come and see me yesterday, although I visited you only the day before. That is not the way to treat a person of my standing.'

These people impose on others to such an extent that no one can endure them, for they are too selfish by far. They are so busy loving themselves that they have little love left for others. Besides, as I said before, people are expected to behave in such a way that each can derive whatever pleasure he may from the other's company. But associating with these difficult persons, whose friendship is lost as easily as a fragile veil can be torn, is more a matter of giving them service than of keeping them company and is therefore not a pleasure but a real burden. So let us leave such delicate feelings and whimsicalities to women.

## CHAPTER II

*Topics of conversation which should be avoided because they may give offence*

MANY faults of various kinds are committed in conversation. First, the topic for discussion should not be trivial or sordid, because instead of giving it their attention and finding pleasure in it, the listeners will despise both the speaker and his argument. Neither should you choose a subject which is too subtle or intricate, because most people will find it difficult to understand. You must take the greatest care not to speak of matters which will cause embarrassment or shame to anybody who is present, and you should beware of coarseness in any form, because however amusing such things may seem to be, honourable people should only use honourable means of pleasing others.

Nothing must ever be said against God or the saints, either seriously or in jest, however witty or entertaining it may be. This was a fault very frequently committed by the high-born characters of the *Decameron*, and they richly deserve to be censured for it by all intelligent people. Remember that to take the name of God in jest is not only sinful and impious, but it is also a breach of good manners. It is painful to listen to, and you will find that many people shun the company of those who speak profanely of God.

And not only should you use God's name with reverence, but in all you say try as far as possible to avoid saying anything which may be held against you or your conduct, for people detest in others even the faults of which they themselves are guilty. In the same way it is inadvisable to talk inopportunely of matters which imply criticism of those who hear them, even though they are harmless in themselves and it would be right and good to mention them at the proper time. Do not therefore repeat the sermons of Fra Nastagio to young ladies who want to enjoy themselves, like the good man who lived near San Pancrazio, not far from your home.[1]

At parties and at mealtimes you should not tell sad stories or say anything to remind people of pain, illness, death, disease, or other distressing subjects. If anyone else lapses into a topic of this sort, you should gently and tactfully change the subject and suggest something more cheerful and more suitable. Even so, as I once heard said by one of our neighbours, a man to be depended on, men often have as much need of tears as they have of laughter. He used to say that this was why the grim plays, which were called tragedies, were first compiled, and the purpose of them when they were recited in the theatres, as was done in those days, was to move to tears all those who felt the need of them. In this way, by weeping, they were cured of their disorders. But, however this may be, it is not right for us to grieve the hearts of the people to whom we are talking, especially on occasions which are meant for happiness and recrea-

---

1. See the *Decameron*, third day, fourth tale. Puccio di Rinieri, who lived near San Pancrazio in Florence, was so devout and abstemious that instead of making love to his wife he would read her Fra Nastagio's sermons on continence.

tion and not for tears. And if you should know of anyone suffering from anxiety to weep, it is very easy to dose him with strong mustard or place him in a smoky room. Therefore there can be no excuse for the theme of misery and death which Filostrato propounded to his companions, whose only desire was for merriment.[1] It is better to remain silent than to talk of matters which cause sorrow.

Equally unpardonable are those people who can never talk of anything but their children, their wives, and their nursemaids. 'My son made me laugh so much yesterday' they say. Or 'Listen to this . . . you never saw a sweeter child than mine . . . My wife is just like that . . . Cecchina said . . . Of course you would never believe it, with a head like hers.' No one has enough time on his hands to listen to such nonsense or to reply to it, and everyone finds it a nuisance.

CHAPTER 12

*The reprehensible habit of telling one's dreams*

WE must also find fault with those people who take every opportunity to tell us of their dreams and do so with such feeling and such amazement that it is quite exhausting to listen to them, especially since they are generally the sort of people whose finest achievements would make dull listening, even if they had been awake when they performed them. We ought not therefore to bore others with such paltry

1. Filostrato, who was president on the fourth day of the *Decameron*, proposed that the tales for that day should be love stories with tragic endings.

matters as dreams, especially if they are fatuous, as they usually are. Of course I have often heard that the books left to us by the wise men of the ancient world contain a great many dreams full of meaning and beauty, but this does not mean that ordinary people like ourselves or the man in the street should follow their example in our conversation. Indeed, of all the dreams that have ever been told to me – and I am not a willing audience – I think that only one was worth the hearing. It was a dream which came to that good gentleman of Rome, Flaminio Tomarozzo, who was by no means uninstructed or unimaginative but was an enlightened man of shrewd intelligence. He dreamed that he was seated in the house of one of his neighbours, a rich chemist. After he had been there a little while, for some reason or other the mob began to riot and set about looting everything. They seized the pills and potions, some taking one thing and some another, and swallowed them there and then, so that in a short time there was not a phial or a jar, a beaker or a bowl, that was not drained dry. Only one little flask, full of a clear liquid, remained, and though many of the people put it to their noses none would dare to taste it. Presently there came upon the scene an old man of great stature and venerable appearance. He looked around gravely at the chemist's bottles and gallipots, which were empty or spilled and for the most part broken, until his eye fell upon the small flask which I have mentioned. He lifted it to his lips and at once drank all the liquid until not a drop remained. Then he went out of the house just as all the others had done.

Flaminio was greatly intrigued by this and turning to the chemist asked 'Master chemist, who is this man and why did he drink all the liquid in the flask with such relish after all the others had refused it?' 'My friend', replied the chemist, 'that was Almighty God. The water which, as you saw, He alone drank and everyone else rejected was discretion, which men will not taste at any price, as perhaps you are aware.'

Dreams of this sort may certainly be told. They are both delightful and instructive to listen to, because they are more like the musings of a lively mind or, shall we say, more like the true faculty of perception than the visions of a sleeper. But other dreams without shape or sense, such as come to most of us, should be forgotten and dismissed with the sleep that brings them, for we who are mean and untutored are neither so wise nor so good as men who are virtuous and learned, even when they are asleep.

## CHAPTER 13

*On the need to avoid exasperating others with
lies, boasting, and false modesty*

ALTHOUGH it might seem that nothing could be vainer than a dream, yet there is one thing even more unreal, and that is a lie. For the things which a man sees in his dreams have some shadow of reality, as though he had experienced them in some way, whereas lies are not the effect either of shadows or of hallucinations. There is therefore even less excuse for stuffing the heads and ears of our audience with lies than with dreams, even though lies may sometimes be taken for the truth. In the long run liars are not only discredited, but no one listens to them any more than they listen to people whose words are meaningless, as though their speech were so much empty breath.

Of course you will find that many liars have no bad intentions. They seek neither profit for themselves nor hurt or scandal for others, but tell lies simply for the love of it, like a man who drinks not for thirst but out of fondness for wine. There are others who tell lies from vainglory, boasting what fine fellows they are and claiming wonderful things of themselves.

Lies may also be told tacitly, that is, by deeds and actions. For instance, you must have seen people who belong to the middle or lower classes of society and yet behave so pompously and arrogantly and speak, or rather lay down the law, with such an assumption of authority, setting themselves up as judges and giving themselves airs, that the very sight of them is more than can be borne.

There are others who are no better off than the rest of us but wear so many gold necklaces, so many rings on their fingers, and so many brooches pinned to their hats and here and there about their clothing, that Castiglione[1] would disown them. Their manners are full of affectation and conceit, resulting from vanity and the pride engendered by it, both of which are undesirable and obnoxious propensities which we should do well to avoid. In many of the best-governed cities the law forbids the rich to wear clothes very much more gorgeous than the poor can afford, because the poor feel themselves outraged when others make a show of their superiority, even if only in appearance. We should therefore take the very greatest care not to fall into these foolish habits.

A man should never boast of his birth, his honours,

1. Baldassare Castiglione, whose book *Il Cortegiano* lays down rules of etiquette in behaviour and dress for the ideal courtier.

or his wealth, and still less of his brains, neither should he make a fine tale of his talents and the great things he has done, recounting them whenever he has a chance, as many people do. If he does so, it will look as if he wishes to throw out a challenge to such of his hearers as are, or claim to be, of the same degree of nobility, riches, and accomplishments as himself, or else it will appear that he wants to show his superiority over those of them who are lesser men than he by making them conscious of their inferiority and their shortcomings. In both cases his behaviour is offensive. No one should therefore either degrade himself or boast, but it is better to detract a little from one's merits than to add to them by talking, because even one's good qualities can displease others if they are overdone. You must also realize that people who make too little of themselves in their talk, and refuse to accept the honours which are obviously their due, show far greater pride in their way than those who claim honours which they have not rightly earned. For this reason it might be said that Giotto did not deserve so much praise as some think, since he would not allow himself to be called master, although he was not only a master of his craft but without doubt a very exceptional one for those days. Whether he deserved praise or blame, it is quite certain that if a man scorns the things which others value it is because he reproaches or despises them for their ambitions; and to disdain the fame and honour which they value so highly is the same as to claim for oneself greater honour and glory than any-one else, because no man in his senses refuses the things which are dear to him, unless he thinks he is already abundantly provided with other things which he values still more. We should therefore neither boast of our blessings nor affect to despise them, for to boast of them would be to reproach others for their faults and to despise them would be to show disdain for their good qualities. Instead, everyone should as far as possible be silent about himself, unless under the circumstances he cannot avoid it, in which case the right thing is to tell the truth modestly, as I said before.

This is why those who wish to be pleasant to others must do all they can to avoid the common habit of making such a pretence of shyness in giving their opinion on anything that it is a mortal torture to listen to them, especially if they are in fact sensible, intelligent persons. 'My dear sir', they will say. 'You must forgive me if I cannot answer you as you would wish. I speak only as a layman and in general terms, with little knowledge of the subject. I am sure you will laugh at me, but I will try to oblige you.' They make such heavy going of it that the most subtle problems might have been resolved in far fewer words and in less time, for they never get to the end of it.

Equally tedious and hypocritical, both in speech and behaviour, are those who assume a role of self-abasement and degradation. Although they are obviously entitled to precedence and a place of honour, they set themselves in the background and it is an unparalleled task to get them to move forward, for they keep stepping backwards like a shying horse. With these people there is always a difficult problem when they come to a doorway, because nothing on earth will make them go through first. They step sideways and backwards, protesting and parrying with their hands and arms, so that at every few paces it is necessary to join battle with them and thus disorganize the proceedings, whether they be pleasure or business.

## CHAPTER 14

*Standing on ceremony – Why ceremonies,
or compliments, are so called, what they are and
how they should be used*

WE use a foreign word, as you can tell from the sound of it, when we speak of ceremonies, just as we do for other things for which there is no word in our own language. This shows that our ancestors knew nothing of such things, for they could find no name for them. Now, in my opinion, because of their emptiness such formalities are little different from the lies and dreams which we have found reason to discuss, so we can well include them under the same head.

As I have often been told by a man of repute, the rites which priests perform on the altar and during their holy office, before God and His holy things, are properly called ceremonies. But when men first began to pay respects to one another with affected and inappropriate mannerisms, such as calling each other 'Sir' or 'Mister', bowing, raising their hats, giving each other pretentious titles, and kissing hands as though they had the consecrated hands of a priest, someone named these new and foolish customs 'ceremonial', for until then they had been without a name. I think he did so for fun, just as drinking and revelry are playfully called a 'carousal', which is certainly not a native word of our own but a foreign barbarism lately imported into Italy, from wherever it may have been. Our poor country, which has been debased and humiliated in the course of events, is puffed up and honoured only in empty words and superfluous titles.

If, then, we consider the intentions of those who

use them, we must conclude that these formalities are a meaningless exhibition of honour and respect paid to the person who is the object of them, consisting of humbug and make-believe by means of stilted titles and lip-service. I say they are meaningless in so far as we make a show of honouring persons whom we do not respect at all but may even despise, and yet, to conform with convention, we call them 'My Lord' or 'Sir' and sometimes even express ourselves as the 'humble servants' of those to whom we would rather do an injury than a service.

These formal expressions may therefore be not only insincere, as I have explained, but even deceitful and fraudulent. But since they have lost their true meaning, as a knife becomes blunt, from the continual use we make of them, we should not take them so literally or put the same strict construction on them as we do with other words. The truth of this is shown by something which happens to all of us every day, for if we meet someone we have never seen before and for some reason are obliged to speak to him, we prefer to say too much rather than too little, and without calling his rank in question we call him 'Sir' or 'Mister', though he may be only a cobbler or a barber dressed in his best clothes. Titles were originally granted by the Pope or the Emperor as a special distinction and could neither be ignored without disrespect or insult to their holders nor attributed except for derision to those who had no right to them. But nowadays these titles and other marks of respect of the same sort should be used more liberally, because convention, which is a hard master, confers these privileges on a great number of men. Despite its fine appearance, then, this custom really means nothing and consists of form without substance and words without sense. But this does not entitle us to alter it. Indeed we are obliged to observe it, albeit with discretion, not through our own fault but for the sake of convention.

## CHAPTER 15

*The three kinds of compliment — Those paid out of self-interest are unworthy of polite persons*

WE must realize that compliments are paid either for one's own benefit or from obsequiousness or because they are right and proper. Every lie told out of self-interest is deceitful, sinful, and dishonest, for lies can never be told honestly. Flatterers commit the same sin, because they pretend to be our friends and pander to our wishes, whatever they may be, not for the purposes we intend but so that we may be of use to them. They do it not to please us but to deceive us, and however pleasant the process may seem to be, it is nevertheless despicable and harmful and quite out of keeping with good manners, because it is wrong to injure anyone by gratifying his humours. If we were right when we said that compliments were a sham and a hollow form of applause, every time we use them to gain our own ends we behave like traitors and swindlers, and therefore they should never be used for these purposes.

## CHAPTER 16

*A warning against neglecting to give honour where it
is due – Precautions to be observed in doing so – The
obligations and exactions of etiquette – Extravagant
adulation is unworthy of honourable people, being the
third kind of compliment, paid for the sake of vanity
– The irritation and tediousness of adulation*

I MUST now speak of compliments which are paid
from good manners and of those which are paid
from vanity. The first kind must on no account be
neglected, because to do so is not only disagreeable but
also offensive. It has often happened that swords have
been drawn because a man has failed to greet a fellow-
townsman in the street with the honours due to him.
This is because convention is all-powerful and in such
matters is taken to have the force of law. For this
reason a man who addresses another as 'you' is not
paying a gratuitous compliment, unless the other is
from the very lowest class of society; but if he were
to call him 'thou', which is the customary way of
speaking to the populace and the peasantry, he would
detract from the other's rights and it would be rude
and insulting.

Other nations and other generations may have had
different customs, but we have these and it is useless
to discuss which are the better. We must subscribe
not necessarily to the best customs but to those which
prevail in our day, just as we obey laws which may
be far from good until the government, or whoever
has power to do so, has changed them. We should
therefore carefully acquaint ourselves with the manners and expressions which modern usage requires for
entertaining, greeting, and speaking to various sorts

of persons in the country where we live, and these are the conventions we should observe in our relations with other people.

Although the Admiral,[1] following the custom which happened to prevail in those days, frequently said 'thou' when he was talking to King Peter of Aragon, we should address our kings as 'Your Majesty' or 'Your Royal Highness', whether we are speaking or writing. We must fall in with the practice of our own times just as he complied with the etiquette of his day.

These are what I call obligatory formalities, because they are not paid of our own accord by our own free choice but are required of us by rule, that is, by common convention; and where there is no question of doing wrong, but it is only a matter of decorum, it is better and indeed right to follow the usual customs without questioning them or quarrelling with them.

Although it is strictly correct to give a kiss, as a sign of reverence, only to the relics of saints and other objects of piety, nevertheless, if it is the custom in your country when taking leave of someone to say 'Sir, I kiss your hands' or 'Your humble servant' or even 'Your slave in chains', you must not be less courteous than others, but when you part company with anyone or write to him, you should address him and take your leave of him, not in the way that reason suggests, but as etiquette demands. Do not say 'Whose master is he, that I should call him "Sir"?' or 'Has this fellow been appointed my parish priest, that I should kiss his hands?' This is because a man who is accustomed to being addressed as 'Sir' and to address others himself in the same way will take it as an affront and a slight if you simply call him by

1 Rugger dell'Oria. See the *Decameron*, fifth day, sixth tale.

his name, or speak to him as 'Mister' or as 'you' right from the start.

These words such as 'Sir' and 'servant' and others of the same kind have lost a great deal of their force, as I have already told you. Like herbs steeped in water they have become weakened and their strength has been dissipated by being so long on the tips of men's tongues. There is no need to recoil from them like those pedantic purists who think that letters written to emperors and kings should begin 'If you and your sons are in good health, all is well. I, too, am in good health,' for they say that this was the way in which the Romans began the letters which they wrote to their government at Rome. If we were to look to the past as these people want, we should gradually revert to living off acorns. But even with these formalities of etiquette certain precautions must be observed, in case we should seem conceited or pompous.

First of all we must take into account the place where the other person lives, because not all usages are acceptable everywhere. Perhaps the customs in vogue in Naples, which is crowded with people of noble stock and titled big-wigs, would be out of place in Lucca or Florence, where the people are mostly merchants and simple burghers without a prince, a marquis, or a baron amongst them. If the stiff and stately manners of Naples were transferred to Florence they would be profuse and exuberant, like a giant's clothes on a pygmy, just as Florentine manners would be meagre and inadequate for the nobility of the Neapolitans and even for their temperament.

If the gentlemen of Venice pay inordinate court to each other on account of the offices they hold and for the sake of their votes, it does not follow that the good people of Rovigo or the citizens of Asolo should observe the same ritual of mutual admiration, and all to no purpose – though, unless I am mistaken, the people of those parts are a little over-fond of such attitudinizing, perhaps out of idleness or because they copy their overlords at Venice, since every man is ready to follow in the footsteps of his leader, even if he does not know the reason why.

Besides this we must take time into consideration as well as the age and status of the other person in relation to our own. When people are busy you should exclude formalities altogether or at least make them as brief as possible. They should be implied rather than expressed. This is an art at which the courtiers of Rome are very adept, though in some other places formalities are a great hindrance to business and exceedingly tedious. Imagine a man told by a busy judge, whose time is precious, to put on his hat. With a few preliminary bows and much shuffling of the feet he eventually replies 'My lord, I am well enough without it'. 'Nevertheless,' says the judge, 'put it on.' After a few contortions to left and to right, bowing to the ground, the other replies with great earnestness 'May it please your Lordship to permit me to do my duty'. This passage at arms lasts so long, with so much waste of time, that the judge might almost have completed all his morning's business in the meanwhile. This shows that although it is the duty of less important people to show respect to judges and other persons of rank, nevertheless, since it is tiresome to persist when time is short, the formalities should be avoided or curtailed.

It is also undesirable for young people to use the same formal behaviour among themselves as older people do, for it is unnatural in them, nor is it suitable for the lower and middle classes to adopt the manners of the aristocracy.

Men of great wisdom and intelligence do not usually pay many of these polite compliments, nor do they like them or expect them of others, for they do not care to exercise their minds on frivolities. Workmen, too, and ordinary people should be careful not to treat important personages with too much ceremonial, which is more likely to irritate them than otherwise, since they look for and expect obedience rather than homage. For this reason it is wrong for a servant to make a show of offering his services to his master, for the master would resent it, thinking that the servant meant to doubt his right to exact obedience and give orders.

These acts of courtesy ought to be performed unstintingly, because services rendered as an obligation are accepted as a due and little gratitude is felt for them, whereas a man who does a little more than is expected of him gives an impression of generosity and is liked for it and considered open-handed. I recall having heard it said of one of the Greek sages, a great poet, that he used to say that a man who could humour others reaped much profit from small capital. You should therefore pay compliments in the way that a tailor makes clothes, cutting a broad hem rather than a narrow one, but not so broad that what was meant for a sock turns out to be a sack or a cloak. If you treat your inferiors with a little appropriate kindness, your chivalry will be acknowledged, and if you do the same to your superiors, they will say you are polite and well behaved. But if you are prodigal and extravagant with your praises, you will be condemned as a frivolous trifler, or perhaps even worse, as a scheming flatterer and what I have heard learned men call a parasite. Unless I am wrong, this was the defect which our forefathers called unctuousness, and there is no fault more obnoxious or less becoming in a gentleman. I have now described the third sort of compliment, the kind which we pay of our own free will and not as a mere convention.

Let us, then, remember what I said at the beginning, that these formalities are not an intrinsic part of human nature. In fact we could have done very well without them, as we did for the most part in our country not so very long ago. But we have been infected with the diseases of others, including not only this infirmity but many others as well. Therefore merely to satisfy the requirements of convention means something quite insignificant, a kind of white lie; but to go further is wrong and cannot be permitted, which is the reason why it is distasteful and intolerable to men of discrimination, who do not find food for their thoughts in frippery and pretences.

I ought to tell you that when I was preparing this treatise, since I had little faith in my own slight knowledge, I sought the opinions of several learned men and found that once upon a time a king named Oedipus, who had been turned out of his own country, went to seek refuge at Athens at the court of King Theseus, because he was being pursued by his enemies. When he came into the presence of Theseus, he heard one of his own daughters speaking and, recognizing her by her voice (for he was blind), in his haste to embrace the child, as a father would, he omitted to pay homage to the king. As soon as he realized his mistake he began to apologize and ask to be forgiven. But the good and wise king interrupted him and said, 'Take heart, Oedipus, for I do not seek honour in the words of others but in my own deeds'. You should remember this pronouncement, for although men are very pleased to be honoured by others, nevertheless, when they perceive that the honour is insincere, they find it tiresome and, furthermore, take it as an insult, because praise, or rather flattery, as well as being evil and repulsive has the additional failing of showing plainly that the flatterer thinks that the person he is wooing is vain and proud besides being a buffoon, a dupe, and a simpleton whom it is easy to impose upon and deceive. Empty, pretentious, and extravagant compliments are undisguised flattery, and in fact they are so obvious and easy to recognize that people who use them to gain some advantage for themselves, besides being dishonest as I have already told you, are also odious and tiresome.

## CHAPTER 17

### *On other vain and inept urbanities, which are the sign of a shallow mind and an ignoble nature*

THERE is another kind of person fond of stylish ceremonial, making a science and a business of it by chapter and verse. At one sort of person they will turn up their noses, to another they will smile, and the highest must sit on a chair, the lowest on a bench. I think this ritual was transplanted to Italy from Spain, but our soil does not suit it and it has not taken firm root, because these precise distinctions of caste are distasteful to us. No one should therefore set himself up as judge to decide who is the nobler and who the more obscure.

Neither should applause be traded in the way that

harlots trade their caresses, as I have noticed in the households of many princes, who make a point of paying their unfortunate retainers with commendations instead of wages.

It is certain that people who like to carry ceremonial to excess do so from empty-headedness and conceit, like the useless persons they are. Since these gallantries are very easily learned and have a certain superficial gracefulness about them, they take great pains to study them. But they are incapable of learning important things, for the burden would be too great for them, and they like conversation to be made up entirely of such prattle, not knowing anything better, like fruit which has a glossy skin, but no juice, and is rotten and mouldering to the touch. For this reason in their relationship with others they dislike to penetrate beyond the façade. You will find such people very numerous.

There are others who make a lavish use of fine words and fine behaviour to make up for their own wrong-doing and the defects of their shabby and miserly dispositions, thinking that no one could abide them if they were as mean and surly in their talk as they are in their dealings.

Truth to tell, you will find that it is more often for one of these two reasons than for any other that people overdo these superficial gallantries, which are generally disliked because they prevent other people from living their lives as they wish, that is in freedom, which everyone prizes above all else.

## CHAPTER 18

*On scandal-mongering, contradicting, giving advice,*
*rebuking others, and correcting their faults, all of*
*which are sources of annoyance*

YOU must not speak ill of other people or their
affairs. Although it may seem that people are glad
to give an ear to such talk, because most of us envy
each other's good fortune and good name, in the end
everyone keeps clear of a kicking horse and we all
distrust the friendship of backbiters for fear that they
may say the same of us behind our backs as they say
of others to our faces.

Those people who dispute every statement by
questioning and contradicting show that they have
little understanding of human nature, because everyone likes to have the upper hand and hates to be
worsted no less in argument than in practice. Besides,
it is the part of an enemy rather than a friend to take
the opposite side. It follows that anyone who wants
to be friendly and pleasant to talk to must not be too
ready to say, 'It was not at all like that' or 'Let me
just give you the true facts', nor should he stake a
wager on the matter. Instead, if the question is of
little importance, he should make an effort to submit
to the opinions of the others, because a point gained
in cases of this sort will turn to his own disadvantage.
This is because we often lose our friends through out-
witting them on small points and making ourselves
so tiresome to them that they dare not have anything
to do with us for fear of a continual bout of contro-
versy. Then they give us the nickname of Fire-eater,
Crosspatch, Wise Bird, or Know-all.

If it sometimes happens that you are invited by your

companions to argue a point with one of them, you should do so quietly and not be so eager for the fruits of victory as to make your opponent eat his words. Everyone should be allowed to have his say and, right or wrong, he should submit to the opinion of the majority or the most importunate and leave the field of battle to them, so that it may be someone else who has to argue and sweat and wear himself out, which is unseemly in a well-behaved person and also inadvisable, for it earns him unpopularity and ill-will. Besides, it is objectionable just because of its impropriety, which is enough in itself to cause annoyance to persons of good taste, as perhaps we shall see later. On the other hand, most people are so enamoured of themselves that they pay no regard to the wishes of others, and in order to demonstrate their own subtlety, intelligence, and wisdom, they will give advice, remonstrate, argue, and take up the cudgels, agreeing to no decision but the one they put forward themselves.

To offer advice without being asked for it is the same as to tell the other person that you are wiser than he is, or even worse, to rebuke him for his stupidity and ignorance. You should therefore not offer advice to every acquaintance but only to your closest friends or to persons whose guidance is in your hands and of whom you have charge or, of course, to anyone, even a stranger, if he is in great danger. But, in general, you should refrain from giving advice to others or trying to make up for their defects. This is a trap into which many fall, most often those who have least judgement, since blunt-witted people have few thoughts in their heads and waste no time in reflection, having few alternatives to choose between. However this may be, anyone who proffers advice and hawks it about is obviously convinced that he has a surplus of common sense while others lack it. There are certainly some people so delighted with their own wisdom that not to follow their advice is much the same as to pick a quarrel with them. They say, 'Very well; the advice of the poor is not accepted', or 'So-and-so wants to do as he thinks best', or 'He will not listen to me', as though it were less presumptuous to expect others to take our advice than for them to insist on following their own.

A similar offence is that committed by people who undertake to correct the faults of others and rebuke them, claiming the final word of judgement on everything and laying down the law for everybody. 'You should not do that.' 'You ought not to have used that word.' 'Stop behaving and talking like that.' 'The wine you are drinking is bad for you. You should drink red wine.' 'You ought to take this mixture and those pills.' Their corrections and reproaches never come to an end. To listen to them is far too great a mortification, not to mention that while they are intent on weeding the other man's garden their own is quite full of prickles and nettles. No one will venture to be friendly with them for the same reason that few people, if any, could abide to live with their doctors or their confessors or still less with a criminal judge. This is because they deprive us of liberty, which everyone wants, and make us feel as though we were in the presence of a preceptor. It is, then, an unlovable habit to be so prompt in correcting and instructing others. It should be left to schoolmasters and fathers to do this and, as you know, for the very reasons I have given you, their charges are ready enough to desert them.

## CHAPTER 19

*On ridicule, which should on no account be used –
How it differs from joking, which should also
generally be avoided – Precautions to be taken in
joking – Two kinds of wit – Biting wit must
never be used*

No one should ever be ridiculed, however great an enemy he may be. You show greater contempt by ridiculing a man than by insulting him, because insults are given in fits of anger or covetousness, and no one gets angry about things which he considers unimportant nor does he covet things which he despises. This shows that you have some respect for the man you insult, but none or very little for the man you ridicule. Ridicule means taking pleasure in putting others to shame, with no advantage to ourselves. It is therefore a point of good manners to avoid making fun of anyone, and it is wrong of people to reprove others for their faults either by what they say, like Forese da Rabatta who laughed at Giotto's appearance,[1] or by their actions, as many do when they mimic stutterers or cripples or hunchbacks. It is just as wrong to mock people who are deformed or freaks or midgets or undersized, or to make merry and raise a laugh when someone makes a foolish remark. Some people, too, delight in making others blush. Despicable behaviour of this sort is deservedly loathsome.

Much the same as these people are the jokers, that is persons who enjoy playing tricks and teasing everyone, not in derision or contempt but for fun. There is no difference between ridicule and joking

1. See the *Decameron*, sixth day, fifth tale.

except in purpose and intention, the distinction being that jokes are made for the sake of amusement while ridicule is meant to hurt. In common speech the two words are very often given the same meaning, but a man who jeers at another takes pleasure in his victim's disgrace, while the joker, who finds amusement but not gratification in another person's mistakes, might well be pained and feel sorry if the same person were made to feel ashamed. Although I made little progress with my studies when I was a boy, I can still remember that although Micio was so fond of Aeschinus that he marvelled at it himself, he would nevertheless sometimes amuse himself by poking fun at him, as he did when he said in an aside, 'Why should I not play a trick on him?'[1] Identical words spoken to one and the same person might be either a jest or a jeer according to the intention of the speaker, and since our purpose may not be obvious to others, it is unwise to behave in their company in so doubtful and suspicious a manner. It is better to avoid the reputation of being a wag than to court it, because just as in games and at play one person may strike another for fun and the blow may be taken seriously, so it often happens that a person who is teased in a friendly way for amusement may resent it and feel himself humiliated and disgraced. Besides, joking is a form of deception and everyone naturally dislikes being wrong and being deluded. So it seems that there are many reasons why anyone who wants to make friends and be liked should not make himself too much of a jester.

It is certainly true that we are quite unable to live our weary mortal lives entirely without recreation and repose, and since jokes are a source of gaiety and

1. *Quor non ludo hunc aliquantisper?* See Terence, *Adelphi*, IV, 5.

laughter and consequently of recreation, we like people who are genial and humorous and amusing. It would therefore seem that there is something to be said for the opposite point of view, that it may sometimes also be proper to be facetious and witty when we are in company. Without doubt those who can crack jokes in a kind and friendly way are more likeable than those who neither do so nor know how to, but it is essential in this matter to bear many things in mind. Since it is the humorist's intention to seek amusement in the failings of someone for whom he has some respect, these failings must not be of the kind which carries any real disgrace or causes him any grave harm. Otherwise it might be difficult to distinguish jokes from insults. There are also some people who are so cantankerous that you should never sharpen your wits on them, as Biondello found out from Messer Filippo Argenti in the Loggia de' Caviccioli.[1]

Similarly, jokes should never be made about serious things or depraved conduct because, as the common saying goes, people will turn vice into comedy, like Filippa of Prato who profited much by the gay replies she gave when she was questioned about her infidelity.[2]

This is why, in my opinion, Lupo degli Uberti did not mitigate his guilt but even increased it by using a pun to excuse his wickedness and cowardice, for

1. See the *Decameron*, ninth day, eighth tale. Ciacco, wishing to avenge himself on Biondello for a trick, sent an offensive message to Filippo, saying it had come from Biondello. Later, when Biondello approached Filippo in the Loggia de' Caviccioli, he was soundly beaten.

2. See the *Decameron*, sixth day, seventh tale. When Filippa da Prato was accused of infidelity to her husband, she answered the charge with such wit that everyone in court laughed and demanded her acquittal.

although he could have held firm in the castle of Laterina, he weakly gave in when he found himself besieged and hemmed in, saying that wolves were not accustomed to stay in cages.[1] Puns and jokes are inappropriate wherever laughter is out of place.

## CHAPTER 20

*Particular remarks on wit, which should be neat and subtle, and being a faculty of the astute, should not be essayed by persons who have no natural disposition for it – How everyone may know whether or not he has a talent for pleasing others with his wit*

YOU must also realize that wit may be either biting or harmless. On this score I should like you to accept Lauretta's wise recommendation, that wit should be like the nibble of a sheep rather than the bite of a dog, for if it were to bite like a dog it would not be witty but insulting.[2] In nearly all cities the laws demand severe punishments for those who grossly insult others, and perhaps it would be right in the same way to prescribe no gentle penalty for those whose wit is unduly biting. Courteous people should assume that the law which covers insults

1. The Uberti were a powerful family in Florence during the twelfth and thirteenth centuries. The incident related here took place in 1288, when Lupo degli Uberti was besieged in the castle of Laterina by the Guelphs. This passage is taken almost word for word from Villani's *Istorie Fiorentine*, book 7, chapter 119. The pun is in the name 'Lupo', which in Italian means 'wolf'.

2. See the *Decameron*, sixth day, third tale, which was told by Lauretta.

applies to wit as well, and they should bite others with it only gently and on rare occasions.

Besides all this you should realize that wit, whether it is biting or not, gives the hearer no pleasure unless it is subtle and neat. He is more likely to be bored by it, or if he laughs, it is not at the quip but at the wag who makes it. Sallies of wit are nothing but tricks of illusion, and since illusion requires delicacy and skill, it can only be effected by astute people who have a ready inspiration and, above all, it must be unexpected. Therefore wittiness does not suit stolid people with obtuse mentalities nor, for that matter, everyone with a good head on his shoulders, like Boccaccio, for instance, whom perhaps it did not suit very well, for it requires a special kind of promptitude, neatness, and immediate mental reaction.

In this matter, therefore, sensible people consider not their inclinations but their aptitude, and when they have tried the strength of their wit once or twice in vain, they recognize that they have little talent for it and cease even to wish to exert themselves on such ventures, in case the same should happen to them as befell Oretta's knight.[1]

If you give some thought to the way in which many people behave, you will easily appreciate that what I tell you is true, in other words that wit does not suit everyone who wants to be witty but only those who have a talent for it. You will find that some people are ready to cap every word with one – or indeed several – of those senseless rhymes which are called jingles. Others will change the syllables of words in an inept and stupid fashion, or say something or

[1]. See the *Decameron*, sixth day, first tale. The knight attempted to entertain Oretta by telling her a story, but told it so badly that she asked him to desist.

answer you in an unexpected way without any subtlety or elegance, such as

> 'Where is he?' 'On his feet.'
> 'He greased their palms with alms.'[1]
> 'Where am I to go?' 'To blazes.'[2]
> 'I want to shave.' 'Then set your face against it.'
> 'Go and call Barbieri.' 'What shall I call him?'

You can easily see that these repartees are cheap and trashy, like most of the jests of Dioneo.[3]

But it is not our task at present to discuss the degrees of elegance in wit, since there are other books on this subject written by far greater experts and better authors than myself, and also because the means of judging whether humour is diverting or irksome are extremely ample and clear, so much so that you cannot mistake them unless you grossly deceive yourself, for when wit is entertaining it provokes immediate gaiety and laughter and a kind of astonishment. So, if your jokes are not rewarded with laughter by your hearers, you must restrain yourself from making any more, for the fault is yours and not theirs. People are tickled by smart remarks and repartee, if it is neat and subtle, and they cannot help laughing even if they wish, but do so in spite of themselves. Just as though they were a just and lawful jury, no one should appeal to his own judgement against theirs or make a further trial of himself.

Furthermore, it is not right to say or do anything cheap or unseemly, such as pulling faces and striking poses, in order to make other people laugh, for no

---

1. and 2. These two phrases, in the original, are taken from the *Decameron*, first day, sixth tale, and sixth day, second tale. Like the other examples of fatuous repartee given here, they cannot be translated exactly as they were written without losing such little humour as they are meant to convey.

3. In the *Decameron*, fifth day, tenth tale.

one should debase himself to please others, which is the trade of clowns and jesters not of dignified persons. You must not therefore follow the low and vulgar example of Dioneo with his song addressed to Aldruda, nor pretend to be insane or eccentric. But those who can should at the proper time say something original and in good taste, the sort of thing that would not occur to everyone; those who cannot should keep silence. Such remarks, if they are made with grace and charm, are a sign and a token of the speaker's active mind and accomplished manners, which are qualities that particularly please others and endear us to them. But if grace and charm are lacking, the result is the opposite, for it will seem like a donkey playing tricks or a fat and full-bottomed man dancing and capering in his shirt-sleeves.

## CHAPTER 21

*On protracted speaking – Rules for telling stories
in an unlaboured style which will please the hearer*

THERE is another way of entertaining others with our conversation, not by means of witty remarks, which are generally brief, but by relating something to them at greater length. Such speeches must be well arranged and expressed, with descriptions of the conduct, demeanour, dispositions, and habits of the people of whom you are talking, so that the audience may be given the impression, not of listening to a tale, but of seeing the action unfold before their eyes. Boccaccio's men and women characters knew very well how to do this, though sometimes, if I am not mistaken, they impersonated their parts more thoroughly than is desirable for ladies and gentlemen, like actors on the stage. If you are to do this, the details of the incident or story, fact or fiction, which you set out to relate, must be assembled in your mind, and you must be prepared with the right words, so that you do not continually have to say 'the thing' and 'the person', or 'what's his name' and 'what do you call it', or 'how can I put it?', or 'what did I say his name was?', for this was precisely the gait of Oretta's knight.

If you are relating some occurrence in which several persons take part, you must not say 'he said' and 'he replied', because we are all 'he' and your listeners will easily be muddled. The story-teller should therefore give his characters names and keep to them. He should also be careful to omit details which add nothing to the charm of the tale or even improve it by being left out. Let me give you an example.

'So and so, who was the son of the man who lived in the Via del Cocomero – surely you know whom I mean? The one who married Gianfigliazzi's daughter, the skinny girl who used to go to Mass at San Lorenzo? You must know him, in fact I am sure you do. A fine old fellow, very erect, with long hair – surely you remember him?'

If it is of no importance whether your story concerns this man rather than anyone else, all this lengthy discussion is useless and, in fact, very tedious to the listeners, who are eager and anxious to hear what happened, while you keep them waiting. Dante did much the same when he wrote

> *E li parenti miei furon lombardi,*
> *E mantovani per patria ambidui,*[1]

1. *Inferno*, 1, 68, 69. 'My parents came from Lombardy and were both of them Mantuans by birth.'

because it did not matter at all whether his mother came from Gazzuolo or from Cremona.

A great foreign speaker once gave me some very useful advice about this. He told me that when you are putting your story together and arranging it, you should refer to the characters by nicknames, but when you tell it, you should give them the names of persons. This is because people are given nicknames to suit their characters, but their real names depend on the wishes of their fathers or whoever christens them. In this way a character who was called Skinflint when the tale was thought out would be named Erminio Grimaldi when it was told, that is, if the general opinion of him in your town is the same as what Guglielmo Borsieri heard about Erminio in Genoa.[1] If there is no well-known person to suit your needs in the place where you live, you must set your tale in another town and give the character any name you please.

It is certainly true that we generally listen with greater pleasure and keener imagination to stories about people whom we know, if the incidents fit their characters, than to tales about strangers who are unknown to us. The reason is that if we know that a certain person usually acts in a certain way, we can believe that he has done what we are told about him and we recognize him as the man in question, but this does not happen with strangers.

1. See the *Decameron*, first day, eighth tale, in which Guglielmo Borsieri, a jester, reproves Erminio Grimaldi, a noted miser, for avarice. The Genoese are to the Italians what the Aberdonians are to us.

## CHAPTER 22

*On the need for clarity and the use of the right words
to convey the meaning in all kinds of speech – A
recommendation for each to use his own language
rather than that of the other person – The necessity
of avoiding objectionable and coarse words and of
learning to talk modestly and quietly by guarding
against a rough and ungainly manner of speech*

BOTH in speaking to an audience and in other forms
of discussion you must use terms clear enough for
everyone in the company to be able to understand
them easily, and your words must have both a pleasant
ring and a pleasant meaning. You should say 'belly'
rather than 'guts' if you have to choose between the
two, and where the sense permits you should say
'stomach' rather than 'belly' or 'paunch', because in
this way you will make your meaning clear, instead
of leaving it to implication, and you will spare your
hearers any ugly allusions. I believe that it was to
avoid the ugly implications of this very word that
Petrarch took care to find a different one when he
wrote

> *Ricordati, che fece il peccar nostro*
> *Prender Dio, per scamparne,*
> *Umana carne al tuo virginal chiostro,*[1]

for he did not hesitate to use another figure of speech
when it suited him not to be quite explicit.

And since Dante, who was an equally fine poet, paid
little heed to these precepts, I think that in this respect
little good can be said of him. Indeed I would not

1. From the poem beginning 'Vergine bella', addressed to the
Virgin Mary. 'Remember that it was our sins which caused God to
take human flesh in thy virgin cloister in order to redeem them.'

advise you to take him for your master in the art of elegance, for he himself had no fads and, in fact, I find that in a certain chronicle it was said of him that he 'was rather presumptuous, insolent, and proud of his great wisdom, and being a little brusque in manner, as philosophers are, he was unable to converse easily with laymen'.[1] But to return to our discussion, I repeat that you must express yourself clearly. To do this you must first learn to use the accepted vocabulary of your own language – but not words which are so antiquated that they have become corrupt and obsolete or have been cast aside and rejected like tattered clothing, such as 'durance vile', 'choler', 'needsome', and so on – and second, the words which you use must have a plain meaning, without a double sense, because it is by combining ambiguous words that we make conundrums or, in simpler language, talk in riddles, like this:

> *Io vidi un che da sette passatoi*
> *Fu da un canto all'altro trapassato.*[2]

You should also choose, as far as possible, words which are appropriate to the meaning you wish to convey and cannot so easily be applied to anything else, because in this way the things you describe will appear to take shape, as though they could be pointed out with the finger and not by words alone. It would be more accurate to say that you recognize someone by his features than by his face or his appearance. Dante, too, by saying that the leaden cloaks of the

1. From Villani's *Chronicles*, IX, 134.
2. From a sonnet by Antonio Alamanni. *Passatoi* could mean either 'stepping stones' or 'projectiles', and *trapassato* either 'crossed over' or 'pierced'. The lines could therefore be translated either 'I saw one whose body was pierced right through by seven darts' or 'I saw one who had crossed from one side to the other by seven steps'. The equivocation cannot be rendered in English.

hypocrites were so heavy that their wearers creaked beneath the weight like an overladen pair of scales, painted a truer picture than if he had said 'shrieked' or 'screeched' or simply 'made a noise'.[1] And it is more precise to speak of the 'shivers' of a fever than the 'cold'; or to say that meat which is too fat 'chokes' us rather than that we 'have our fill' of it; or that we 'air' our clothes rather than 'hang them out'; or that a man is 'one-armed' rather than that he has 'lost a limb'. Dante was right to speak of the frogs with their 'snouts' above water at the side of a ditch instead of saying 'their mouths'.[2] All these words have only one meaning. In the same way it is better to say the 'hem' of a piece of cloth rather than the 'side'.

I am well aware that if, as ill luck would have it, some foreigner were to come across this book, he would take me to task and say that I was teaching you jargon or some special code, because most of these words are so idiomatic that they are not to be found in some other languages and foreigners do not understand us when we use them. Who could know what Dante meant by these verses?

> *Già veggia, per mezzul perdere o lulla,*
> *Com' io vidi un, così non si pertugia,*
> *Rotto dal mento infin dove si trulla.*[3]

I am sure that none but a Florentine could understand them. All the same, according to what I have heard,

1. *Inferno*, XXIII, 100–2. *Le cappe rance*
   *Son di piombo, sì grosse, che li pesi*
   *Fan così cigolar le lor bilance.*
2. *Ibid.*, XXII, 25–7. *E come all'orlo dell'acqua d'un fosso*
   *Stanno i ranocchi, pur col muso fuori,*
   *Sì che celano i piedi e l'altro grosso.*
3. *Ibid.*, XXVIII, 22–4. 'No one would even open a barrel, for fear of losing the centre-piece or the two side-pieces in the bottom of it, in the way that I saw one man gashed from his jaws right down to his haunches.'

if Dante had any faults, they did not lie in his choice of words but rather in the fact that, since he was a little headstrong, he undertook to say things which were rather difficult to express in words; and perhaps it was not that he expressed them badly but that they were unpleasant to listen to.

No one, then, can very well talk to anybody who does not understand the language he speaks. But if foreigners do not know our language, we should not for that reason speak it in a broken way when we talk to them, nor should we act as Brufaldo did,[1] like some people who are so foolish as to try to speak the language of the person they are talking to, no matter where he may come from, and say everything the wrong way round. It often happens that a Spaniard will speak to an Italian in Italian, and the Italian, to cut a fine figure, will answer him in Spanish, yet it is much easier to recognize that each is speaking a language not his own than to restrain one's laughter at the fatuous nonsense which escapes their lips.

Let us therefore speak the other person's language or dialect whenever, for some necessity, we need to make ourselves understood clearly, but in common conversation we shall use our own dialect, even if it is less perfect, rather than his, which may be more expressive. For a Lombard will speak his own mother tongue, which varies more than any other from our own, better than Tuscan or any other dialect, because, amongst other reasons, however hard he tries he will never master the idioms and the proper vocabulary as well as we Tuscans do. Furthermore, if anyone, out of consideration for the people to whom he is talking, refrains from using the idiomatic terms of which I have spoken and, instead of them uses words

1. This reference is obscure.

with a more general and less explicit meaning, his conversation will be, for that reason, all the less interesting.

Besides this every cultured person must avoid using indecent words. The words may themselves have an indecent meaning or they may be suggestive of one by reason of their sound or the way in which they are spoken. This is because some words, although their meaning is unexceptionable, nevertheless have an obscene ring about them. The word '*rinculare*'[1] is an example, although it is in daily use by everybody. But if anybody, either man or woman, were to employ a word meaning 'go forward' coined by a similar analogy and in the same way as this one, which means 'go back', the obscenity would immediately become obvious. However, since we are used to this word, our ears are deaf to its suggestive undertone.

Although Dante wrote

*La mano alzò con ambedue le fiche*[2]

our women are shy of using the dubious word '*fiche*'. To avoid it they prefer to say '*castagne*' instead, although very often some who are not on their guard use the word without thinking, and yet they would blush for shame if anyone else were to utter it at random in their presence or swear by this word which denotes their sex. Women who are ladylike, or wish to be so, should therefore see to it that they avoid immodesty not only in behaviour but also in speech, and they should beware not only of words which are indelicate, vulgar, or coarse, but also of those which

1. *Rinculare* is a normal word meaning to 'move back', but the syllable *cul* by itself means 'buttocks'.
2. *Inferno*, xxv, 2. *Fiche*, here used to mean an obscene sign made with the fingers, could mean either 'figs' or the female 'pudenda'. *Castagne* means 'chestnuts'.

may seem to be so, like these words of Dante, which some find indecent:

> *Se non ch'al viso e di sotto mi venta,*[1]

or

> *Però ne dite ond'è presso il pertugio.*

> . . . . . . . .

> *E un di quelli spirti disse: Vieni*
> *Di retro a noi, che troverai la buca.*[2]

You must realize that although there may often be two or more words with the same meaning, some are decent and others less so. It is right to say 'He slept with her' or 'She gave herself to him', because the same thing expressed in other words would be indecent to listen to. And it is more fitting to speak of a lady's 'favourite' than of her 'paramour', though both of these words mean 'lover', and of a man's 'sweetheart' or 'friend' rather than his 'mistress'. Again, when you are speaking to a woman or even to a man of gentle breeding, it is more polite to use the phrase of Belcolore,[3] whose speech was more modest than her actions, and speak of prostitutes as 'women of the world' rather than call them by their proper name, as Dante did when he said '*Taide è la puttana*'.[4] Boccaccio's words, too, when he spoke of 'the influence of courtesans and boys'[5] would have been indecent and shameless if he had use the proper term for the boys as he did for the women.

Moreover, you must be on your guard not only against gross and indecent words, but also against

1. *Inferno*, XVII, 117. 'Were it not that I felt the wind on my face and beneath me.'

2. *Purgatorio*, XVIII, III, 113, 114. 'Tell me where the passage is. . . . And one of the spirits answered, Come along behind us and you will find the cleft.'

3. See the *Decameron*, eighth day, second tale.

4. *Inferno*, XVIII, 133.

5. See the *Decameron*, first day, second tale.

those which lack dignity, especially when you speak of grand and noble things. For this reason perhaps Beatrice deserved some blame when she said

> *L'alto fato di Dio sarebbe rotto,*
> *Se Lete si passasse, e tal vivanda*
> *Fosse gustata senza alcun scotto*
> *Di pentimento, che lagrime spanda* [1]

for, in my opinion, the low language of the pot-house was out of place in this splendid passage. No one should say 'the lantern of the world' [2] instead of the 'sun', because this word is associated with the smell of oil and cooking, and no thinking person would say that St Dominic was the 'suitor of my lady Theology', nor would he say that the glorious saints had used such abject words as

> *E lascia pur grattar dove è la rogna,* [3]

which are sullied with the dregs of vulgarity, as anyone can tell without difficulty.

When you have to speak for any length of time, therefore, you must bear in mind the points I have mentioned as well as some others, which you can more easily learn from your masters by studying the art which they are accustomed to call rhetoric. At other times you must learn to use words which are polite, modest, and agreeable, with no unpleasant savour about them. You should say, 'I did not explain myself very well' rather than 'You do not understand my meaning', and 'Let us just think whether what we say is true' rather than 'You were wrong' or 'It is not

---

1. Dante, *Purgatorio* XXX, 142–5. 'God's high justice would be stayed if men could pass through Lethe and enjoy its draught without making payment by shedding tears of repentance.' 'Scotto' is the word for payment made to an innkeeper.

2. 'La lucerna del mondo.' Dante, *Paradiso*, I, 38.

3. *Ibid.*, XVII, 129. 'Lets them scratch where the pox tickles.'

so' or 'You do not know', because it is a polite and friendly custom to excuse others even when you know that the fault is theirs. In fact, when your friend makes a mistake, you should share the blame and take some of it upon yourself before complaining about it and rebuking him. You should say 'We mistook the way' or 'We forgot to do such and such yesterday', even when he was the only one who forgot. When Restagnone said to his companions, 'If what you say is true',[1] he was ill-mannered because it is not right to question the good faith of others. If anyone has promised you anything and has not kept his promise, you ought not to tell him that he has broken his word, unless you are obliged to do so for a good reason in order to save your own good name. But if he has tried to cheat you, you can say, 'You did not remember to do such and such', and if he has simply forgotten, you should say 'You could not do it' or 'It slipped your memory', instead of 'You have forgotten' or 'You did not trouble to keep your promise'. Remarks like these have a sting and are tainted with the venom of spite and meanness, so that people who habitually say such things earn themselves a bad name for bitterness and disagreeability and others shun their company, just as they would keep clear of prickles and thorns.

1. See the *Decameron*, fourth day, third tale.

## CHAPTER 23

*More remarks about speaking – Take good stock of
the subject before beginning to talk – How to control
the voice – The arrangement of words – A warning
about pompousness and vulgarisms – Let your
manner of speaking be suitably restrained*

I HAVE known some of those people who have the
bad and irritating habit of being so eager and
anxious to have their say that they overlook the trend
of the argument and outstrip it, coursing ahead like
greyhounds which do not catch their quarry. For this
reason I will not shrink from telling you something
which might seem superfluous to recall because it is
so obvious, that is, never to speak before you have
set out in your mind what you are going to say. In
this way you will give birth to sound reasoning and
not to some abortion – and any stranger who may
trouble to read this poor screed will surely permit me
to use this word. If you take my advice seriously, you
will never find yourself saying 'Good morning,
Agostino' to someone whose name is Agnolo or
Bernardo, and you will never have to take back your
words or say 'I was wrong' or 'How stupid of me to
say so!', nor will you have to stammer and stutter
while you search for the right word. It is a real torture
to hear someone say 'Arrigo – no, that's not right.
Is it Arabico? That's it! Agabito!'

The voice should be neither hoarse nor gruff. It
must not be shrill, nor creak like a pulley-wheel, either
with laughter or for any other reason. No one should
continue to speak while he yawns. You know very
well that we cannot acquire at will either a fluent
tongue or a good voice, and therefore anyone who

stammers or croaks should forgo the attempt to be a chatterer and try instead to overcome the defects of his tongue by keeping silence and using his ears, and he can also reduce his natural impediments if he tries. It is bad manners to shout like a town crier, but neither should you speak so quietly that you cannot be heard. If you are not heard the first time, you must not repeat yourself in an even quieter voice, nor must you shout; for, if you do, you will appear to be angry at having to say all over again what you had said before.

The words must be arranged in the order required by common speech, not shuffled about here and there in the way that many people speak because they think it clever. They sound more like lawyers reading translations of deeds drawn up in Latin than men talking in their own language. To say such things as

> *Immagini di ben seguendo false,*[1]

or

> *Del fiorir queste innanzi tempo tempie,*[2]

is a style which is sometimes allowed to poets but can never be permitted in common conversation.

In ordinary speech a man must avoid not only flights of poetry but also the bombast of oratory. Otherwise he will be dreary and dull to listen to, even though it may be that formal speaking displays greater ability than ordinary conversation. But there is a proper time and place for it, just as the street is the proper place for walking, not for dancing, for everyone can walk, though not all can dance, and dancing is suitable for weddings but not for the street. You

1. Dante, *Purgatorio*, xxx, 131. 'Following false visions of delight.'
2. From Petrarch's sonnet beginning *Non da l'hispano Hibero*. '[Laura does not see that] my temples are grey before their time.' In both these passages the words are misplaced to suit the rhyme and metre.

must therefore guard against speaking pompously like Titus[1] in the *Decameron* or in the style of the *Filocolo* and all the other works of Boccaccio, though we must make an exception for his greatest work, the *Decameron*, and perhaps even more so for the *Corbaccio*.

This does not mean that I want you to learn to talk the coarse language of the dregs of the populace, like a washerwoman or a street-hawker, but as well-bred persons do, and I have already in part told you how this can be done, that is, by not mentioning subjects which are low or paltry, gross or repugnant; by selecting the purest and most accurate words in your own language and those which both sound right and have the right meaning, without ugly, vulgar, or base associations; and by assembling them in such a way that they are neither piled up haphazard nor set out in an order which is too obviously premeditated. Besides this you must take care to arrange all that you have to say without discrepancy and avoid placing together expressions which are inconsistent, such as

> Cicero and Linus and Seneca the moralist,[2]

or

> One was from Padua, the other a layman.[3]

You must talk neither too slowly, as though you had lost your taste for speech, nor too avidly, as though you were ravenous for it, but composedly as a sober man should. You must pronounce each letter and

---

1. *Decameron*, tenth day, eighth tale.
2. Dante, *Inferno*, IV, 141. *Tullio e Lino e Seneca morale.* The author objects to the name of a character from mythology being grouped with those of Cicero and Seneca. An alternative reading of Dante's text gives the name of Livy instead of Linus.
3. *L'uno era padovano, l'altro laico.* From Burchiello's sonnet beginning *Io vidi un dì.*

syllable unobtrusively, not like a schoolmaster teaching children to read and write, and not mouthing them or running them together in a tangled jabber. If you remember these points and others like them, people will listen willingly and with pleasure to what you have to say, and you will keep the honourable position which a polite, well-brought-up person should have.

## CHAPTER 24

*On verbosity – People who want to do all the talking, and those who interrupt others – Various faults committed in this way – Reasons why it is displeasing to talk too much and also disagreeable to be too taciturn*

THERE are also many people who cannot stop talking. Like a ship which is driven on by its own speed and does not heave to when the sails are furled, they run on carried away by the force of momentum and do not even come to a standstill when their arguments are exhausted, but either repeat what they have already said or prattle emptily on.

Some others are so agog to talk that they will allow no one else to speak. Just as in the farmyard you will sometimes see one chicken grab a grain of meal from the beak of another, in the same way these people take the words out of a speaker's mouth and begin to talk themselves. They surely give the other person every reason to want to pick a quarrel with them because, if you think it over, nothing moves a man to anger so much as a sudden check to his wishes or his pleasures, however trifling, such as when someone blocks your mouth when you open it to yawn or unexpectedly holds your arm when you raise it to throw a stone.

Actions like these and many others of the same sort, which are likely to interfere with another person's intentions and pleasures, are exasperating and should be avoided, even when they are done for fun and in good part. The same is true in conversation, for you should not interfere with another's wishes but try to make things easy for him instead. When someone is on the point of recounting a piece of news, you should not spoil it for him or say that you know it already. And if he allows a few untruths to slip into his story, you must not reproach him for them either by what you say or by such gestures as shaking your head or making a wry face. People often do these things in the pretence that they cannot possibly endure the misery of a lie, but the real reason is that the malice and bitterness of their own tart and quarrelsome natures makes them so spiteful and acrimonious in the company of others that no one can abide them. In the same way it is an irritating and unpleasant habit to interrupt other people when they are speaking, for it is much like holding a man back when he starts to run.

It is also wrong, when someone is talking, to do anything to distract those who are listening and draw them away from him, by pointing out something else and turning their attention to other things, for no one has the right to dismiss another man's guests. You must also pay attention when a person is speaking, so that you are not obliged to keep saying 'What did you say?' or 'What was that?'. This is a common fault, as much of a nuisance to a speaker as pebbles are to a man who stumbles on them when he walks.

If there is a halting speaker, you must not move ahead of him or find his words for him, as though you had plenty to spare for his needs. Many people take this amiss, especially those who are convinced that they are good speakers, because they are made aware that you do not share their own opinion of themselves and that you want to help them at their own craft. They are like businessmen who consider it a disgrace to have money offered to them, as though they had none themselves and needed it from other people because they were poor. You should realize that everyone thinks he can talk well, though some pretend not to out of modesty.

I cannot imagine why it should be that those who know least talk most. Polite people should be careful not to talk too much, especially if their knowledge is small, not only because it is very difficult to talk a lot without making a lot of mistakes, but also because the speaker enjoys a position of superiority, as it were, over his hearers, like a master among his pupils, and it is not right that he should assume more than his fair share of this superiority. Many people fall into this fault, not only individuals but whole nations of glib and tedious talkers who are the ruin of all whose ears they seize upon.

It is offensive to be too silent just as it is irritating to talk too much, because not to join in the conversation when others are talking seems to show that you do not want to foot your share of the bill, and also because by speaking you open your mind to those who listen, whereas by keeping silence you appear to want to remain a stranger. This is why reticent people are unwelcome in cheerful and friendly company, just as in countries where they drink a lot and get merry at their revels it is usual to exclude people who do not drink. So the proper way to behave is for everyone to wait his turn both for speaking and for keeping silence.


## CHAPTER 25

*The author tells the story of a sculptor, and apologizes for not being able to put his own precepts into practice – He next encourages his pupil to form good habits while he is still young – He points out the virtues of reason and its power over our instinctive appetites, and sums up what has been said so far*

ACCORDING to a very ancient chronicle, there once lived a good man in Greece, a sculptor called Polycleitus, which was a name given to him, as I believe, on account of his great renown. When he was an old man he drew up a treatise in which he gathered together all the golden rules of his art, which he knew to perfection. He showed how the limbs of the body were to be measured, both by themselves and in relation to each other, so that they should be in the proper proportions. He called his work the 'Rule', meaning by this name that the statues which other sculptors made from that time onwards should be shaped and designed according to it, in the same way as beams, masonry, and walls are gauged with a rule. But it is much easier to say things than to do them and put them into practice, and furthermore, since most people are quicker to feel things than to understand them, especially those of us who are ordinary men with no special knowledge, we more readily learn from object-lessons and examples than from general principles and propositions or, in plain language, from reason. So Polycleitus, in his wisdom, realizing that craftsmen were by their nature unlikely to profit much from general guidance, decided to make the value of his lessons even clearer. He took a block of fine marble and with great labour made from it a statue which agreed in every limb and in all its parts with the principles which he had laid down in his book, and he called it the 'Rule' just as he had named the book.

Now may God be pleased to allow me to achieve, at least in part, one of the two things which this great master of sculpture did so perfectly, that is, to gather together in this book the proper rules of the art which is the subject of my discourse. As for the other, the second Rule which he made, which for me would be to observe and adhere to these maxims in my own behaviour and make myself into a living example of them, as if I were a statue plain to see, it is now beyond my powers; for where the manners and customs of society are concerned, it is not enough to know the theory and the rules but, in order to put them into effect, it is necessary to acquire the habit as well, and this cannot be done in a moment or in a short space of time. It needs many, many years and my remaining years are few, as you can see. But this is no reason why you should place less faith in the advice I give you, for a man may well point out to others the course he took when he lost his way and, in fact, it may well be that those who have gone astray have a better memory for the wrong and misleading paths than those who have kept to the right road.

If those who had charge of me in childhood, when the mind is tender and yielding, had known both how to tame my manners, which were naturally rather blunt and rough, and how to soften and polish them, perhaps I should have become such a man as I am now trying to make of you, who are no less dear to me than if you were my son. For however great the power of our natural inclinations may be, they are very often overcome and corrected by the rules of behaviour. But we must start early to pit ourselves against them and repel them before they assert themselves and grow too strong for us. So far from doing this, most people drift along without control, following wherever their instincts lead them, and thinking that they are obeying the laws of nature, as though reason were not natural in a man. Yet reason is our mistress, with the power to change bad habits and to come to the aid of nature and raise her up if ever she should lurch or fall. But most of us do not listen to her voice, and so for the most part we are like the beasts to whom God did not give the gift of reason. Yet reason has some power even over animals, not their own reason, for they have none themselves, but ours. You can see this happen with horses, which would often, indeed always, be wild by nature, and yet their master tames them and even makes them seem almost like reasonable and well-behaved persons. For though many of them would trot at an awkward pace if left to themselves, the trainer teaches them to step lightly and also to stand still and run and turn and jump, and they learn how to do it, as you know.

Now if horses, dogs, birds, and many other animals even wilder than these will submit to a man's reason and obey it and learn things which they could not know by nature, but would even resist; and if, not by instinct but by training, they become, as you might say, good and wise as far as it is in them to be so, how much more likely is it that we should become better under the guidance of our own reason, if we gave it our ears? But our senses tell us to crave for and enjoy the pleasure we see before us, whatever it may be, and they shrink from trouble and stave it off. This is also why they recoil from reason, which seems harsh to them because instead of pleasure, which is often harmful, it offers us our own good, which always requires an effort and tastes sour to a spoiled palate. As long as we live according to the senses, we are like a pitiful invalid to whom all food tastes bitter and salty, however dainty and sweet it may be. He complains of his servant or his cook, who are quite blameless, because the bitterness is not in the food but in himself and on the tongue with which he tastes it. In the same way reason, which in itself is sweet, tastes bitter to us, not because of its own flavour but because of our lack of relish. This is why, being fastidious and finicky, we refuse to taste it and excuse our faults by saying that there is no spur or rein to check nature or drive her on. And yet I am sure that if oxen or donkeys or even pigs could talk, they could put forward no more wretched and inept argument than this.

We should still be children even in our prime and in ripe old age, and greybeards would behave as aimlessly as babies, were it not that reason grows in us with the years and, once it has grown, turns us almost from animals into men. For it is even stronger and more powerful than our natural instincts and appetites, and if our lives and our behaviour are bad, it is not through the fault of reason but because of our own wickedness.

It is untrue then that natural tendencies cannot be

restrained or mastered. On the contrary, there are two means, by reason and by good manners. But, as I told you before, bad manners cannot be changed into good by reason alone. Good manners must also come from habit, and habit is the child of time. So we must start early in life to listen to the voice of reason, not only because in this way we have a longer time in which to get used to being the kind of people she teaches us to be, and to be familiar with her and loyal to her, but also because children, in their innocence, are more easily impressed and the things we get used to first always please us the most. This is why they say that Theodorus,[1] who was a great master of the art of producing plays, always wanted his own to be staged first even though the other actors, who were to perform before him, were unlikely to win much applause; for he did not want his words to fall upon ears already attuned to other voices, less eloquent than his though they may have been.

Since, for the reasons which I have given you, I cannot suit my conduct to my words like Polycleitus, who could apply his lessons as well as teach, let me content myself with having told you in some part how you ought to behave, for I am unfit to put any part of it into practice myself. But we cannot recognize light unless we also know the dark, and we cannot learn what sound is unless we are also aware of silence, and in the same way, if you take notice of my poor manners, which have but a dim light, you will be able to discover the brilliance which shines in manners which are attractive and exemplary. Now, to return to our subject, which we shall soon bring to an end, let us remember that manners are attractive when they give pleasure to others or, at least, do not

1. A Greek actor of the fourth century.

hurt the feelings or interfere with the wishes of our friends or suggest anything unpleasant to them; and this is what we have spoken about so far.

## CHAPTER 26

*Before explaining which things we should avoid doing because they are mentally disturbing to others, the author points out that men are lovers of beauty and proportion – He defines beauty and shows how it can be found in words and deeds as well as in objects*

BESIDES what we have already said, you ought to realize that men are great lovers of beauty and form and proportion. Conversely they detest things which are ugly, ill-made, and mis-shapen. This is a special gift of man, for the other animals can recognize neither beauty nor any form at all; and since the sense of beauty is ours alone and we do not share it with the beasts, we ought to appreciate it for its own value and hold it very dear, especially those of us who are more sensitive and therefore recognize beauty all the more readily. It is difficult to find words to explain what beauty is, but so that you may have some means of recognizing it, I will tell you that it is to be found wherever the parts of a whole are in due proportion both to each other and to the whole itself, and anything which has these proportions can truly be said to be a thing of beauty.

According to what I was told on another occasion by a wise and learned man, beauty is one whole, a single total, whereas ugliness consists of many single parts. You can see what this means if you consider the faces of girls who are fair and comely, because each of them has features which seem to have been made for her own face and hers alone. But it is not so with girls who are plain, for an ugly girl may have large and prominent eyes, a small nose, puffed cheeks, thin lips, a jutting chin, and a dark complexion, so that her face seems not to belong to one woman only but to be made up of parts taken from the faces of several.

There are also women whose limbs are very shapely if each is seen separately, but ugly and unpleasing in combination, simply because they are all parts of different beautiful women and not only of the one who seems to have borrowed them on loan from all the others. Perhaps the painter[1] for whom the girls of Calabria posed in the nude did no more than recognize which of Venus' limbs each of them had appropriated to herself, and when he had restored each limb to the goddess, she was there ready to be painted, for he could picture to himself her beauty and how it was composed.

Now I do not want you to imagine that this is only true of faces, limbs, and bodies, for the case is exactly the same with speech and behaviour. If you were to see a noble, richly bedecked lady washing her crockery in the gutter at the roadside, even though you felt no other concern for her, you would still find it distasteful to see her in a dual role, for in her own state she would be an immaculate and exalted lady, whereas drudgery is the lot of lowly, unkempt women. There would be nothing about her to offend the senses, no unpleasant taste or smell, no jarring sound or blatant colour, and yet her unbecoming and degrading behaviour and the discrepancy of her task would be enough in themselves to upset you.

1. Zeuxis, of Heraclea, in Lucania.

## CHAPTER 27

*How things which are repulsive to the senses also
upset the mind – Reasons why this is so, in addition
to what has already been said on this subject*

You must therefore also avoid incongruous and ill-contrived behaviour of this sort with as much or even more care than the kind of behaviour I have spoken about so far, for it is harder to recognize this kind of mistake than the other. This is because it is plainly easier to feel things than to understand them. All the same it may often happen that what disgusts the senses also upsets the mind, though not for the same reason as I gave you before. I told you then that a man should dress according to convention, in order not to appear to censure others and correct them, which in most cases would conflict with their wishes, since they look for approval. But it would also offend against the good taste of people who appreciate such things, because clothes which belong to another age do not suit a person who belongs to this one. It is equally wrong to dress like an old clothes man, whose garments fit him so badly that his doublet is obviously at odds with his hose.

Here we could quite well mention again many of the points of which we have already spoken, perhaps all of them, because they were all examples of lack of proper restraint, which is what we are discussing now. The time and place, the things which were done and the persons who did them were all out of keeping and were not made to suit each other as they should have been, for the human mind appreciates and enjoys consistency. But I preferred to marshal them together and arrange them under the banner of the senses, so to speak, rather than assign them to the mind, so that everyone may recognize them more easily. For we are all readily aware of feelings and sensations, but not everyone can understand such abstract notions as these, particularly that which we call beauty, grace, or elegance.

## CHAPTER 28

*A well-mannered person should try to perform every action with grace and decorum – All forms of vice are particularly degrading and are therefore to be shunned – Details of particular matters where a proper restraint must be used, and a special word about clothes*

A MAN must therefore not be content to do things well, but must also aim to do them gracefully. Gracefulness is like a light which shines in things which are fit and proper for their purpose because they are well ordered and arranged both in relation to each other and as a whole. Without it even goodness has no beauty and beauty has no charm. However healthy and nourishing it might be, guests would not like food which had a nasty taste or no taste at all. In the same way manners which are quite harmless in themselves may sometimes be, as it were, insipid and unpalatable unless they are flavoured with something to sweeten them. This, I believe, is what we mean by grace and charm.

This by itself is sufficient reason why all forms of vice are in themselves obnoxious, for vice is ugly and degrading and those who value self-restraint and sobriety are offended and disgusted by the impropriety of it. It follows that the first rule for all who wish to make themselves pleasant to others is to avoid vice, particularly in its nastier forms, such as lechery, avarice, cruelty, and so on. Some vices are despicable, like gluttony or drunkenness; some are shameful, like lechery; some are criminal, like the shedding of blood; and the other vices, some more than others, are similarly repulsive in society, each in its own way and because of its own intrinsic qualities, but all of them without exception make a man unwelcome in the company of others because, as I told you before, they are at variance with it. But since I undertook to point out men's errors to you, not their sins, I must not make it my business to comment on the nature of the virtues and the vices, but confine myself to discussing correct and incorrect behaviour in men's relations with each other. What I told you about Count Ricciardo was a case of incorrect behaviour which the good bishop immediately noticed, just as a well-trained singer will hear a false note, because it was ugly and did not match the rest of his manners, which were graceful and restrained.

Polite people ought therefore to be mindful of the need for restraint such as I have described in their manner of walking, standing, or sitting, and in all that they do, in their gestures and in their dress, when they speak and when they are silent, when they are at rest and when they are at work. This is why a man ought not to embellish himself like a woman, for the adornments would be out of keeping with his sex. Yet I sometimes see men whose hair and beards are curled with hot tongs and whose faces, necks, and hands have been smoothed and titivated more than any young wench would allow, or even any harlot who is more anxious to hawk her wares and sell them at a good price.

There should be no excessive smell about the body, either pleasant or otherwise, in order that a gentleman should not have the odour of a workman nor a man carry with him the scent of a woman or a whore. But at your age I think you may be allowed to use some simple distilled perfumes.

For the reasons which I have already given you, your clothes should follow the fashion of the age you live in and be suited to your condition in life, for conventions are created by time and destroyed again in the same way, and we cannot alter them to please ourselves. But everyone can adapt the fashion to his own needs. For example, if your legs are very long and the fashion is for clothes to be short, you can have yours made rather longer than the very shortest style, and anyone whose legs are too thin, or exceptionally fat, or perhaps crooked, should not wear vivid or parti-coloured hose, in order not to attract attention to his defects.

None of your clothes must be too dapper or too ornate, so that no one may say that you are wearing Ganymede's hose or Cupid's doublet. Whatever you wear, it must suit you and be compatible with your calling. Otherwise a priest might dress like a soldier and a soldier like a jester. When Castruccio Castracane[1] was in Rome with Ludwig the Bavarian[2] in triumphant glory as Duke of Lucca and Pistoia, Count of Palazzo, Senator of Rome, and Lord and Marshal of the Bavarian's court, for the sake of ostentation and display he had made for himself a cloak

1. A famous condottiero, created Duke of Lucca in 1327.
2. The Emperor Louis IV, called the Bavarian, crowned in Rome in 1328.

of crimson velvet, on which were embroidered in front golden letters reading 'It is as God wills', and on the back more golden letters which read 'It shall be as God wills'. I think you will yourself admit that it would have suited his trumpeter better than himself. And although kings are above the law, nevertheless I could not approve King Manfred's[1] custom of dressing in green draperies.

We ought therefore to see to it that the clothes not only suit the wearer but also fit his station in life. Besides this they must be suitable for the place where he lives. For although different places have different systems of weights and measures, in spite of this buying, selling, and trading still take place in each of them, and in the same way, although customs differ from place to place, a man can adjust his behaviour to suit them.

The plumes which Neapolitans and Spaniards wear in their head-dress, and all forms of trimming and embroidery, are out of place in the dress of serious persons and city-dwellers. Armour and chain-mail are still less suitable. Such things may be fitting in Verona, but they are not to be thought of in Venice, for these brocaded gentlemen, with their plumes and their armour, are ill-suited to that venerable city of peace and orderliness. They are like nettles and burrs among the lush plants of a garden, and this is why they are not well received in righteous company, for they are out of keeping with it.

A person of quality should not run in the street or be in too great haste. These are things which a groom may do but not a gentleman. Besides, they tire a man out and make him sweat and pant for breath, which is unbecoming in a person of the better sort. For the

1. King of Sicily, 1258–66.

same reason you should not move as slowly or daintily as a woman or a bride. When you are walking you should not take too great strides, and you should neither dangle your arms nor swing them violently, nor gesticulate as though you were sowing seed in a field. Nor should you stare at anyone's face as though it were something to wonder at.

Some people when they are walking raise their feet as high as a shying horse, as though they were lifting them out of a bran-tub. Others stamp the ground so hard that they make almost as much noise as a cart. One man will give a kick to the side with his foot, another will brandish his leg about or continually stoop to pull up his hose. And there are others who waggle their haunches and preen themselves like peacocks. All these habits are unpleasant because, instead of being elegant, they are just the reverse.

If your horse should happen to hold its mouth open or show its tongue, although this would not affect the animal's efficiency, it would make a very great difference to its value, and you would get much less for it, not because the horse was any the less strong, but because it was so much the less handsome. Again, two houses may be equally well built and furnished, but this does not mean that they can be sold at the same price, for one of them may have good proportions and the other bad. If, then, we appreciate a graceful appearance in animals and even in lifeless objects, which have neither heart nor soul, how much more ought we not to foster it and value it in human beings?

## CHAPTER 29

*Some particular instances of bad table-manners, and in this connexion, some remarks about excessive drinking*

IT is not polite to scratch yourself when you are seated at table. You should also take care, as far as you can, not to spit at mealtimes, but if you must spit, then do so in a decent manner. I have often heard that the people of some countries are so demure that they never spit at all, and we might well refrain from doing so for a short time. We should also be careful not to gobble our food so greedily as to cause ourselves to get the hiccups or commit some other unpleasantness, like a man who hurries so much that he makes himself puff and blow, which annoys everybody else.

It is also bad manners to clean your teeth with your napkin, and still worse to do it with your finger, for such conduct is unsightly. It is wrong to rinse your mouth and spit out the wine in public, and it is not a polite habit, when you rise from the table, to carry your toothpick either in your mouth, like a bird making its nest, or behind your ear. Anyone who carries a toothpick hung on a cord around his neck is certainly at fault, for besides the fact that it is a strange object to see drawn from beneath a gentleman's waistcoat and reminds us of those cheapjack dentists who can be seen in the market-place, it also shows that the wearer is well equipped and provided with the wherewithal of a glutton. I cannot explain why these people do not also carry their spoons tied around their necks.

It is also unmannerly to sprawl over the table or to fill both sides of your mouth so full with food that your cheeks are bloated. And you must do nothing to show that you have found great relish in the food or the wine, for these are the customs of the tavern and the alehouse.

In my opinion it is undesirable to press food on those who are at table with you by saying 'You are eating nothing this morning', or 'Does none of this food tempt you?', or 'Try some of this, or some of that'. Most people think it friendly and hospitable to do this, but although it is their way of showing concern for their guests, it also very often causes the guests to lose their appetite, because they are embarrassed to think that they are being watched.

I do not think it right to offer food from one's own plate to anyone else, unless the person who offers it is of much more exalted rank, in which case it would be a mark of honour for the other. If both are of equal rank, it is rather a presumption of superiority for one of them to offer his food to the other, and sometimes the titbit might not be to his taste. It also shows that the dishes were unfairly served, since one person has too much and the other not enough, and this might embarrass the host. Nevertheless, in this matter we must do as everyone else does, and not as we think right. In conventions of this sort it is better to be wrong in company with others than to be the only one to be right. But whatever may be the rights of the matter, you must not refuse what is offered to you because, if you do, you will appear to despise or rebuke the person who offers it.

The practice of challenging others to drink, which is not an Italian custom and is known by the foreign name of 'brindisi', is in itself reprehensible and has not yet been adopted in our country, which is the reason why you should not do it. If anyone else challenges you, you can easily decline to accept by saying that you admit defeat, and you may thank him and even taste a little of the wine for the sake of politeness without drinking any more.

These drinking bouts were an ancient custom of the Greeks, or so I have heard tell from several learned men, who are full of praise for a good man named Socrates, who lived in those days. He spent the whole length of a night in a drinking contest with another good man called Aristophanes, and at dawn the next day he worked out a difficult problem in geometry without a single mistake. In this way he proved that the wine had done him no harm. The learned also say that by frequently risking his life a man becomes fearless and sure of himself, and in the same way he learns sober and polite habits by growing used to the dangers of intemperance. They claim that drinking wine in this way, in excessive quantities, by way of a contest, is a great trial of the drinker's strength, and that it is done to test his powers so that he may learn to resist and overcome great temptations. Nevertheless, my own opinion is against this and I find these arguments extremely frivolous.

We often find that learned men, by their grandiose talk, can prove that right is wrong and wrong is right. So, in this matter, let us not believe what they say. It might also be that they want to excuse and cloak the evils of their own country, which is corrupted by this vice. Perhaps they might think it dangerous to denounce it, and fear that the same might happen to them as happened to Socrates because he was too much given to pointing out the faults of everyone else. Many charges of false doctrine and other base crimes were brought against him out of jealousy, and he was found guilty of them, trumped up though they were, for in reality he was a good man and true to the idolatrous beliefs of those days. But he certainly deserved no praise for drinking so much wine that night, for a barrel would have done better than he did, since it would have held more. If it did him no harm, it was more likely due to his strong head than to the self-control of a civilized man.

Whatever the ancient chronicles may say about it, for my part I thank God that for all the many other plagues which have come to us from beyond the Alps, this most pernicious custom of making game of drunkenness, and even admiring it, has not yet reached as far as this. I shall never believe that temperance must be learnt from such masters as wine and drunkenness.

The head servant must never take it upon himself to invite strangers to the house or ask them to stay and dine with his master, and no one who has his wits about him will accept an invitation to a meal from such a person, though sometimes servants are presumptuous enough to wish to do of their own accord the things which are the prerogative of their masters. I mention this here in passing, not because it fits into the plan which we first set out to follow.

## CHAPTER 30

*More instances of bad manners and ungainly behaviour
which must be avoided, and with these the book is
brought to an end*

No one must take off his clothes, especially his
lower garments, in public, that is, in the presence
of decent people, because this is not the right place
for undressing. Besides, it might happen that the
parts of the body which are normally hidden should
be laid bare, and this would embarrass both the man
himself and the onlookers.

You should neither comb your hair nor wash your
hands in the presence of others, because – except for
washing the hands before going in to a meal – such
things are done in the bedroom and not in public.
Before meals it is right to wash your hands openly,
even though you have no need to do so, in order that
those who dip their fingers in the same dish as yourself may know for certain that you have cleaned them.

Again, you must not appear in public with your
nightcap on your head or fasten your hose when other
people are present.

Some people have a way of pursing their lips from
time to time, or screwing up their eyes, or puffing
their cheeks and blowing out their breath, or making
various similar grimaces. They ought to desist entirely
from these habits. I was once told by some men of
learning that the goddess Athene used to enjoy playing the bagpipes and had quite mastered the art. It
happened that one day as she was playing them for
pleasure beside a spring she saw her reflection in the
water, and when she saw how she had to distort her
face to blow the pipes, she was abashed and threw

them away. She did well to do this, because the bag-pipes are not an instrument for women, and, in fact, are equally unsuitable for men, except for those poor wretches who are paid to play them and make a trade of it.

What I say about unsightly grimaces applies equally to all the other parts of the body. It is wrong to put out your tongue or stroke your beard too much, which is a common habit. And you must not rub your hands together, or sigh aloud, or groan. Nor must you quiver and shake with excitement, as some people do, or stretch yourself and grunt with sleepiness, like a yokel waking up in a hay-rick.

Anyone who makes a nasty noise with his lips as a sign of astonishment or disapproval is obviously imitating something indecent, and imitations are not too far from the truth.

Laughter must not be a giggle, a roar, or a cackle, and you must not laugh from habit when there is no call to do so. I would not have you laugh at your own jokes, because this is a form of self-praise. It is the hearer who should laugh, not the speaker.

I do not want you to think that since each one of these faults is small, they amount to little when they are put together. The truth is that a grave fault is made up of many lesser ones, as I said at the beginning, and the smaller they are the more important it is to fix one's eye on them, because they are not easy to discern. They creep into our habits before we are aware of them, and just as continual small expenses will quietly eat away a fortune, so these peccadilloes, by mass of numbers, will stealthily destroy politeness and good manners.

A man must also consider how he moves his body, particularly while he is talking, because it very often happens that he is so wrapped up in what he is saying that he has little thought for anything else. Some people wag their heads; others, with their eyes starting out of their heads, will raise one eyebrow half-way up the forehead and lower the other down to the chin; others twist their lips or spit on the clothes and in the faces of the persons to whom they are talking. There are also people who gesticulate as though they wanted to drive away the flies. Such behaviour is ugly and distressing.

As you know, I have had much to do with men of learning, and I once heard that a good man called Pindar used to say that everything which savoured of delicacy and refinement had been seasoned by the goddess of grace and beauty.

What need I say of people who leave their offices and go about with their pens behind their ears? Or of those who chew their handkerchiefs? Or of those who put one leg on the table, or spit on their fingers? Or of innumerable other foolish habits? I could not list them all, nor do I intend to try. Indeed there may be many who will say that even the ones which I have mentioned are too many and to spare.

# A Note on Books of Courtesy in England

A FEW notes on some of the books of courtesy which
our forefathers read may help to place the *Galateo* in
perspective. There is a very wide literature on the subject,
ranging from treatises on ethics to manuals of etiquette,
from tracts and discourses on the cardinal virtues to lists
of do's and don't's for brides and débutantes. Nothing
like a complete survey is possible in a few pages, but it
may be of interest to mention some examples for com-
parison with the *Galateo*, together with some very brief
notes about the kind of people for whom they were
written.

In our enlightened age we are accustomed to look back
upon the period before the Renaissance as a time when
might was right, humour broad, and manners rough and
ready. We need only turn to Chaucer to read of disreputable
characters like the miller, who 'had a store of tavern
stories'.[1] This proves nothing, except that saloon bar
stories have a long tradition behind them. There were
other pilgrims on the way to Canterbury who were at
least presentable.

> There was a Knight, a most distinguished man,
> Who from the day on which he first began
> To ride abroad had followed chivalry,
> Truth, honour, generous thought and courtesy.[1]

And the prioress would surely have done credit to the
most respectable front parlour.

> At meat her manners were well taught withal;
> No morsel from her lips did she let fall,

1. *Canterbury Tales, Prologue*, Nevill Coghill's translation. (Penguin
Classics.)

Nor dipped her fingers in the sauce too deep;
But she could carry a morsel up and keep
The smallest drop from falling on her breast.
For courtliness she had a special zest.
And she would wipe her upper lip so clean
That not a trace of grease was to be seen
Upon the cup when she had drunk; to eat
She reached a hand sedately for the meat.
She certainly was very entertaining,
Pleasant and friendly in her ways, and straining
To counterfeit a courtly kind of grace,
A stately bearing fitting to her place.[1]

Though the nuns and the knights may have been out-numbered by the millers, they nevertheless managed to pass on the traditions of courtesy and chivalry from one generation to the next, and they certainly made some attempt to educate their children in elementary politeness. Several medieval books on manners have survived, many of them intended for children.[2] Provided that he was literate, a young man living in the middle of the fifteenth century might have expected to read some such crude verses as these:

Thou shalt not laugh nor speak nor sing
While thy mouth be full of meat or drink,
Nor sup not with great sounding
Neither potage nor other thing.
Let not thy spoon stand in thy dish,
Whether thou be served with flesh or fish. . . .

Also eschew, without strife
To foul the board cloth with thy knife,

1. *Canterbury Tales, Prologue*, Nevill Coghill's translation. (Penguin Classics.)
2. Probably the oldest extant courtesy-books are Thomasin von Zirclaria's *Der Wälsche Gast*, written about 1210, Bonvicino da Riva's *De le zinquanta cortexie da tavola* (*c.* 1290), and two poems by Francesco da Barberino, *Del reggimento e costumi di donna* and *Documenti d'amore*, dating from the first decade of the fourteenth century. Perhaps the most notable of the English books was the *Babees Book*, translated from a lost Latin poem and intended as a primer on the duties of youths serving in the households of noblemen.

Nor blow not on thy drink nor meat,
Neither for cold, nor for heat.

> (Modernized from the *Boke of Curtasye*, mid-fifteenth century.)

Also keep thy hands fair and well
From fouling of the towel.
Thereon thou shalt not thy nose wipe,
Neither at thy meat thy tooth thou pick.
Too deep in thy cup thou may not sink,
Though thou have good will to drink,
Lest thy eyes water thereby,
Then is it no courtesy.

> (Modernized from a fifteenth-century poem entitled *Urbanitatis*.)

From the fourteenth century onwards the standards which gentlemen set for themselves were influenced by two quite unconnected developments. The first of these was the invention of firearms, which so altered the conception of warfare and the methods of waging it, that the traditional rules of chivalry and the ideal of personal distinction on the field of battle gradually became outmoded. Early in the sixteenth century Ariosto wrote 'How did this infamous and ugly invention ever find a place in human hearts? Because of it the glory of war is destroyed and the profession of arms is without honour, valour and virtue are so debased that evil often seems better than good, and boldness and daring can no longer be put to the test in the field'.[1] This heartfelt lament supplies the reason why Ariosto kept his tongue at least partly in his cheek when he wrote *Orlando Furioso*. It also explains how it was that, within a century, Cervantes was able to mock quite openly at knight-errantry and chivalrous adventure.

The direct connexion between gunpowder and manners is possibly remote, but its invention put an end to a society in which skill at arms was the best qualification for a gentleman. The second development supplied a new ideal

1. *Orlando Furioso*, XI, 26.

to take its place, for rapid progress in the art of printing during the second half of the fifteenth century meant that books were available for all who could learn to read them and study need no longer be the privilege of the Church and the law. In addition to courage and the knightly virtues a gentleman was expected to have some knowledge of literature, particularly the Greek and Latin classics which were again coming to light. The Renaissance has been labelled 'pagan', but it would be a mistake to believe that the revival of secular literature spelt the end of Christian traditions. It did, however, undoubtedly mean the opening of a wide new field of what we nowadays call culture, and culture, of course, includes good manners. One of the most popular books, Cicero's *De officiis*, which is a practical code of social conduct, was printed more than sixty times in various countries before the end of the century, and Seneca was also widely read. Under the influence of books of this sort a new class of educated layman began to appear, endowed with accomplishments not unlike those of Chaucer's squire, who, it will be remembered, could sing, dance, draw, and recite poems as well as he could ride a horse and exhibit his skill at jousting.

The Tudor ideal of a gentleman, 'the courtier's, soldier's, scholar's, eye, tongue, sword',[1] represented by such men as Sir Thomas Wyatt, Sir Philip Sidney, and Saint Thomas More, owed much to the influence of Italian scholarship and culture, which was disseminated in England, not only by returned travellers, but also by large numbers of books translated from the Italian. Something has already been said of one of the most influential of these books, Castiglione's *Cortegiano*,[2] for which the critical Roger Ascham had nothing but praise. Besides the foreign authors English writers also began to devote themselves to the subject of human perfection. This was the purpose which Spenser had in mind when he wrote in the dedica-

1. Shakespeare, *Hamlet*, III, 1.
2. See the introduction, p. 16.

tion of the *Faerie Queen* that 'the generall end . . . of all the booke is to fashion a gentleman or noble person in vertuous and gentle discipline'. The term 'gentleman' now also included a new middle class, the sons of merchants and minor squires, educated in the grammar schools and primed with more refined tastes than those of the lower populace, whose chief interests were drinking, swearing, dicing, cock-fighting, and a murderous variety of football. They learned their behaviour from various books, such as Sir Thomas Elyot's *Governour* (1531), which was the first treatise on education to be printed in England; Thomas Lupset's *Exhortation to Yonge Men, perswading them to walke in the pathe way that leadeth to honeste and goodnes* (c. 1530), which recommended the reading of Cicero, Seneca, and Ovid as well as the Scriptures; and the anonymous *Institucion of a Gentleman* (1555), which advised on suitable occupations and pastimes for the upper classes and gave them hints on choosing their clothes. There were also a number of books dealing specifically with the subject of good behaviour, which was an essential part of a gentleman's training. It would require a great deal of space to deal with them all, but some short extracts from three of them will show that, with some exceptions, their authors insisted on much the same standards as we do.

Ouer moche laughyng is foule and dishonest,
Unto the face and fygure nat smal dyfformyte.
One alway loude laughyng at euery toy and iest
Maketh his hyd folly playne euydent to be.
One euery where laughyng is as a child to se.
Loude gyglyng and laughyng is but a folysshe sygne
And euydent token of maners femenyne.

> (ALEXANDER BARCLAY. *Mirror of Good Manners*, 1523.)

Salt with thy knife reach to and take,
    Thy bread cut fair and no mammocks make.
Thy spoon with pottage too full do not fill
    For fouling the cloth, if it chance to spill.

And rudeness it is thy pottage to sup,
  Or speak to any, his nose in the cup.
Thy knife see be sharp to cut smooth thy meat,
  Thy mouth fill not full when as thou dost eat:
Not smacking thy lips as commonly do hogs,
  Nor gnawing of bones as do dunghill-dogs.
Such rudeness abhor, such beastliness fly,
  At the table behave thyself mannerly:
Thy fingers keep clean thy trencher upon,
  Having a napkin wipe them thereon.

      (FRANCIS SEAGER. *The Schoole of Vertue,*
      1557. Mammocks = fragments.)


Nor imitate with Socrates
  To wipe thy snivelled nose
Upon thy cap, as he would doe,
  Nor yet upon thy clothes.

But keepe it cleane with handkerchiffe,
  Provided for the same,
Not with thy fingers or thy sleeve,
  Therein thou art to blame.

Blow not alowd as thou shalt stand,
  For that is most absurd,
Just like a broken winded horse.
  It is to be abhord.

Nor practise snuffingly to speake,
  For that doth imitate
The brutish storke and elephant,
  Yea and the wralling cat.

If thou of force doe chance to neeze,
  Then backewards turne away
From presence of the company,
  Wherein thou art to stay.

Thy cheekes with shamefac't modesty,
  Dipt in Dame Nature's die,
Nor counterfet, nor puffed out,
  Observe it carefully.

110

Keepe close thy mouth, for why, thy breath
    May hap to give offence,
And other worse may be repayd
    For further recompence.

Nor put thy lips out like a foole
    As thou wouldst kiss a horse,
When thou before thy betters art,
    And what is ten times worse,

To gape in such unseemly sort,
    With ugly gaping mouth,
Is like an image pictured
    A blowing from the south.

Which to avoyd, then turne about,
    And with a napkin hide
That gaping foule deformity,
    When thou art so aside.

To laugh at all things thou shalt heare,
    Is neither good nor fit,
It shewes the property and forme
    Of one with little wit. . . .

To put the tongue out wantonly,
    And draw it in agen,
Betokens mocking of thyselfe,
    In all the eyes of men.

If spitting chance to move thee so
    Thou canst it not forbeare,
Remember doe it modestly
    Consider who is there.

If filthinesse, or ordure thou
    Upon the floore doe cast,
Tread out, and cleanse it with thy foot,
    Let that be done with haste. . . .

To belch or bulch like Clitipho,
    Whom Terence setteth forth,
Commendeth manners to be base,
    Most foule and nothing worth.

If thou to vomit be constrain'd,
    Avoyd from company:
So shall it better be excus'd,
    If not through gluttony.

Keep white thy teeth, and wash thy mouth
    With water pure and cleane,
And in that washing, mannerly
    Observe and keep a meane.

Thy head let that be kembd and trimd,
    Let thy not thy haire be long,
It is unseemely to the eye,
    Rebuked by the tongue. . . .

Let not thy privy members be
    Layd open to be view'd,
It is most shamefull and abhord,
    Detestable and rude.

Retaine not urine nor the winde,
    Which doth the body vex,
So it be done with secresie,
    Let that not thee perplex.

And in thy sitting use a meane,
    As may become thee well,
Not straddling, no nor tottering,
    And dangling like a bell.

Observe in curtesie to take
    A rule of decent kinde,
Bend not thy body too far foorth,
    Nor backe thy leg behind.

(RICHARD WESTE. *The Schoole of Vertue*, the
second part [of the work by F. Seager], 1619.)

During the first four decades of the seventeenth century
life continued very much as before, at least for the upper
classes. They were still intent upon establishing the causes
and the qualities which elevated them above their fellows,
and several attempts were made to supply the answers and
record them in print. Probably the best remembered

efforts were James Cleland's 'Ηρω-Παιδεια *or the Institution of a Young Nobleman* (1607); Richard Brathwait's *The English Gentleman* (1630) and *The English Gentlewoman* (1631); and above all, Henry Peacham's *The Compleat Gentleman* (1622). This book, which was typical of its kind, dealt with a variety of subjects. It began with an analysis of nobility, and went on to discuss education and the duties of parents, how a young man should spend his time at the university, how he should develop his style in speaking and writing, and the value of exercising himself in geography, geometry, poetry, music, drawing, painting, heraldry, and various kinds of sport. The ancients were called to give evidence even in the most elementary connexions, such as particular kinds of games. We are told, for example, that 'leaping is an exercise very commendable, and healthfull for the body, especially if you use it in the morning, as we reade Alexander and Epaminondas did. Upon a full stomacke or to bedward, it is very dangerous, and in no wise to be exercised.'

Peacham did not deal with manners in detail except for guidance on virtues such as temperance and moderation. Later in the century Obadiah Walker, in a book entitled *Of Education, especially of Young Gentlemen* (1673), gave some useful advice on dirty and greedy habits and, cautioning his readers against the formal manners of the French school, uttered some wise and much needed words on the distinction between etiquette and true manners.

Civility consists in these things. 1. In not expressing by actions, or speeches, any injury, disesteem, offence, or undervaluing of any other. 2. In being ready to do all good offices and ordinary kindness for another. And 3ly in receiving no injuries or offences from others, i.e. in not resenting every word or action, which may (perhaps rationally) be interpreted to be disesteem or undervaluing. . . .

Civility is not, therefore, punctuality of behaviour: I mean that which consists in certain modish and particular ceremonies and fashions, in clothes, gesture, mine, speech, or the like; is not using such discourses, words, phrases, studies, opinions, games, &c. as are in fashion in the Court; with gallants, ladies, &c. This is a constrain'd formality, not civility; a complying with the times, not with persons; and varieth with the age or season, frequently according to the fancy of mechanic persons, in their several professions; whereas the rules of civility, founded upon prudence and charity, are to perpetuity unchangeable.

But it was not only from books that the English learned their manners. Records of their attendance at foreign universities go back long before the times of which we are speaking, but during the sixteenth century the habit of travelling for the purpose of acquiring general culture began to grow. William Thomas wrote that there were many foreigners at the university of Padua when he was there in the second half of the 1540s. They were mostly 'gentilmen whose resort thither is principallie under pretence of studie'.[1] But as time went on their thoughts turned to other things besides scholarship. Bacon, in his essay on travel, gave a long list of points worth the traveller's attention, ending with a warning about foreign manners. 'Let it appeare that he doth not change his country manners for those of forraigne parts; but onely pricke in some flowers, of that he hath learned abroad, into the customes of his owne countrey.' This warning was only too often ignored. James Howell, the Historiographer Royal, complained that 'some kind of travellers there are, whom their gate and strouting, their bending in the hammes, and shoulders, and looking upon their legges, with frisking and singing do speake them travellers. Others by a phantastique kind of ribanding themselves, by their modes of habit, and cloathing ... do make themselves knowne to have breathed forraine ayre.'[2]

Of all the countries visited by Englishmen at this time Italy was the favourite. The British have always been suspicious of foreigners, but Howell thought that there was less risk of learning bad habits in Italy than elsewhere. 'One shall learne besides there not to interrupt one in the

1. *Historie of Italie*, 1549.
2. *Instructions for Forreine Travel*, 1642.

relation of his tale, or to feed it with odde interlocutions: one shall learne also not to laugh at his own jest, as too many use to do, like a hen, which cannot lay an egge but she must cackle.'[1] As for the danger of learning such mannerisms as 'strouting' or 'frisking', it is only fair to the Italians to say that such novelties were not their own creation but had largely been imported into their country from Spain.

The Italians, in fact, were supposed to have the best manners in Europe. They even used forks at their meals, 'because the Italian cannot by any means indure to have his dish touched with fingers, seeing all men's fingers are not alike cleane'.[2] In England such delicacy was rare, as we hear from Ben Jonson.

> *Sledge*: Forks! What be they?
> *Meercraft*: The laudable use of forks,
> Brought into custom here, as they are in Italy
> To the sparing of napkins.[3]

Fynes Moryson, the Elizabethan traveller, who visited Italy in 1593–95, found the manners of the Italians exemplary, though not in every particular.

Touching the manners of the Italians. They are for the out syde by natures guift excellently composed. By sweetnes of language, and singular art in seasoning their talke and behaviour with great ostentation of courtesy, they make their conversation sweete and pleasing to all men, easily gayning the good will of those with whome they live. . . . They are affable at the first sight, but no long accquaintance can make them famillier, much lesse rude in behaviour, as some other nations are, who being familiar, yea perhaps litle or not at all acquainted, will presently call men by nicknames, yea being their superiours, as Tom, Jack, Will, Dic, and the like, yea will leape upon their frendes shoulders, and if they wilbe merye, presently fling coushions, stooles, yea custardes or whatsoever is next hand, one at anothers head, and thereby many tymes fall from sport

1. *Instructions for Forreine Travel*, 1642.
2. *Coryat's Crudities*, 1611.
3. *The Devil is an Ass*, v, 4. 1616.

to earnest quarrals. This kind of familiarity Italians hate above all others, and thincke it a manifest signe of a barren witt, falling to such sporte for want of ability to discourse. . . .

To conclude, as the Italians in generall are of exquisite behavior, so I have seene many of them in some particular things, very unmannerly, as in frequent using beastly wordes as interjections of exclamation or admiration. . . . Agayne it is not rare, espetially at Venice and Padoa, to see an Italyan setting on the closestool and talking with his chamber fellowes while they are eating.

(From Shakespeare's Europe, unpublished chapters of Moryson's Itinerary, edited by Charles Hughes, 1903, but not included in the original, which was published in 1617.)

The custom of sending young men to study abroad, much as young ladies were later sent to learn deportment in continental finishing schools, became very popular during the seventeenth and eighteenth centuries. This was what came to be known as the 'Grand Tour', and though in the latter half of the eighteenth century it was no longer taken quite so seriously, it retained its devotees until the French Revolution altered the social structure of Europe. During the seventeenth century France took the place of Italy as the most important country on the route, and countless young men from England learned to behave themselves, under the care of a tutor, in the best French society and in special academies, where they were instructed in languages, riding, fencing, dancing, and other polite accomplishments.

After the Restoration English social life was much influenced by the example of France, partly at least through Charles II's connexions with the French court. From this time until the Revolution France was supreme on the Continent and, naturally enough, English Court circles imported from across the Channel a somewhat frivolous and cynical attitude to virtue, which was reflected in fashionable life and has been recorded for us in the drama of the period. The French had developed a code of polite conduct regulated to suit all occasions and all degrees of society. It is not surprising that some of their books were translated into English. The works of the Abbé Bellegarde, for instance, became very popular in England at the beginning of the eighteenth century, but there were several others available before then. A Frenchman, Jean Gailhard, who 'hath been tutor abroad to several of the nobility and gentry', wrote in English a comprehensive book called *The Compleat Gentleman* (1678), dealing particularly with the advantages of foreign travel. Shortly before this, in 1671, a book entitled *The Rules of Civility*, translated from Antoine de Courtin's *Nouveau traité de la civilité*, had detailed the correct etiquette for all sorts of occasions including visits, musical soirées, and journeys in stage coaches. It also gave instruction on correct modes of address both in speaking and in writing letters. This is what the author has to say about behaviour in the ballroom:

If you be at a ball, you must know exactly (if not how to dance) at least the rules observed in dancing. . . . If your talent at that exercise be not great, you must not pretend to more skill than you have, nor ingage yourself in dances that you understand but little, if anything at all. If your ear be bad, you must not undertake to dance, though you step never so well; it renders a man ridiculous to see him out in his time; and the rather because it is his own fault, for, if he needs must come to the ball, he might have excus'd himself for dancing, by making a profound congy to the lady that took him out, having first conducted her into the middle of the room.

Probably the most memorable book translated from the French at this time was the anonymous *Bienséance de la conversation entre les hommes*, originally published in French in 1595 and translated into English with the title *Youth's Behaviour* by Francis Hawkins about 1640. Its contents were very largely based on the *Galateo*, as can be seen from the following extract:

Sing not with thy mouth, humming to thyself, unlesse thou be alone, in such sort as thou canst not be heard by others. Strike not up a drum with thy fingers, or thy feet.

Rub not thy teeth nor crash them, nor make any thing crack in such manner that thou disquiet any body.

It is an uncivill thing to stretch out thine arms at length, and writhe them hither and thither.

In coughing, or sneezing, make not great noise, if it be possible, and send not forth any sigh, in such wise that others observe thee, without great occasion.

In yawning howl not, and thou shouldst abstain as much as thou canst to yawn especially when thou speakest, for that sheweth one to be weary, and that one little accounted of the company; but if thou be'est constrained to yawn, by all means, for that time being, speak not, nor gape wide mouthed, but shut thy mouth with thy hand, or with thy handkerchief if it be needfull, readily turning thy face to another side.

When thou blowest thy nose, make not thy nose sound like a trumpet, and after that look not within thy handkerchief. . . .

It is not decent to spit upon the fire, much lesse to lay hands upon the embers. . . .

Gnaw not thy nails in the presence of others, nor bite them with thy teeth.

Spit not on thy fingers, and draw them not as if it were to make them longer: also snifle not in the sight of others.

Neither shake thy head, feet, or legs; rowl not thine eyes. Lift not one of thine eye-browes higher than thine other. . . .

Spit not far off thee, nor behind thee, but aside, a little distant and not right before thy companion: but if it be some grosse flegme, one ought, if it may be, tread upon it.

The period between the Restoration and the industrial revolution is usually thought of as the golden age of the aristocracy in England. Elegance was the order of the day, in manners and dress as well as in literature and art. We like to think of it as the period of Sir Roger de Coverley and Sir Charles Grandison, as though these characters were representative of their age instead of being pictures of the 'might have been'. Elegance indeed there was, but it was a studied pose, a caricature of the ideals put forward in the earlier gentlemen's books. Manners were largely play-acting and the part of each actor was carefully studied beforehand. This was too good a target for Swift to miss. His *Complete Collection of Genteel and Ingenious Conversation* (1738) exposed all the tricks of the trade. It contained three model dialogues of the greatest refinement, with the suggestion that readers should commit them to memory for use on suitable occasions. John Gay, too, in a passage which gives advice on good manners in the streets, had a gentle laugh at the young buck about town.

> Let due civilities be strictly paid.
> The wall surrender to the hooded maid;
> Nor let thy sturdy elbow's hasty rage
> Jostle the feeble steps of trembling age:
> And when the porter bends beneath his load,
> And pants for breath; clear thou the crouded road.
> But, above all, the groping blind direct,
> And from the pressing throng the lame protect.
> You'll sometimes meet a fop, of nicest tread,
> Whose mantling peruke veils his empty head;
> At ev'ry step he dreads the wall to lose,
> And risques, to save a coach, his red-heel'd shoes;
> Him, like the miller, pass with caution by,
> Lest from his shoulder clouds of powder fly.
> But when the bully, with assuming pace,
> Cocks his broad hat, edg'd round with tarnished lace,
> Yield not the way; defy his strutting pride,
> And thrust him to the muddy kennel's side;
> He never turns again, nor dares oppose,
> But mutters coward curses as he goes.

> (From *Trivia; or, The Art of Walking the Streets
> of London*, 1716.)

Probably the best remembered book on manners produced in the eighteenth century was Chesterfield's *Letters to His Son*, published in 1774, soon after the author's death. The fact that it became immediately popular shows that there was still a public sincerely interested in the proper virtues of a gentleman. But Chesterfield was the last of the old school. Many of the nobility and gentry were now more interested in wearing fine clothes and building country mansions than in living up to their social obligations. They still sent their sons abroad to study comportment, but foreign travel was now more a fashionable pastime than a serious attempt to gain an education. Foreigners were regarded as curiosities, no longer as models of etiquette, and their influence on English social habits declined as the wealth and self-esteem of Britain grew. In fact the boot was gradually being shifted to the other foot and a certain anglomania was already discernible in some continental circles. French fashions, as ever, were popular and, in a minor way, some people were still prepared to ape continental customs, like the 'macaronis' or the literary set who gathered around Lady Anna Miller at Batheaston, where assemblies modelled on the French salons and the Italian conversazioni were regularly held to encourage would-be writers of elegant verse.

But the elegant silver cloud was not without its black lining. If we read between the lines of an anonymous book called *The Man of Manners* (about 1735), we can see that the manners of the beaux were not always as fine as their clothes.

It is become allowable at all polite tables, to wash one's mouth, or gargle after meals: tho' very uncivil to pick one's teeth with the knife or fork, because it looks like a Lyon's Inn lawyer at the end of his dinner, in the long vacation. . . .

To proportion our cloaths to our bodies, is a thing few people observe, and yet very essential to our being neat and becoming; and indeed without that, we do but make ourselves ridiculous. As for instance, a man with a complexion as pale as a virgin lady's chamber-pot, to wear a perriwig as white as a double-refined sugar-loaf. . . .

'Tis convenient to keep one's eyes, and particularly the teeth wash't and clean. I have known the ladies watch a man in the mouth, as careful as the most skilful jockey does a horse in Smithfield Market, to see whether he was deficient or not in this respect; we ought likewise to cut our nails constantly, tho' not to spend all our time upon them, as the Inns-of-Court beaus do in the coffee-houses. . . .

To sleep in company is vastly unbecoming a person of sense and good manners, and ought never to be indulg'd, except when anyone is telling a long ridiculous story.

Another book which gives a glimpse of the real truth behind the elegant façade was Roger Bull's new translation of Friedrich Dedekind's *Grobianus, or the Complete Booby*, published in 1739. This work was originally published in Germany in 1549 and had previously been translated into English in 1605, but Bull's verses are neater than those of the earlier version. The poem is an ironic glorification of bad manners and much of its humour is of a gross, Germanic kind, but here are some samples of the less indelicate lines:

> When air imprison'd labours for a vent,
> That you should belch, I give my free consent:
> Nor belch to halves, but of the clangor proud,
> Like some substantial burgo-master, belch aloud. . . .

> To cut your nails is neither meet nor right;
> Long nails are ever grateful to the sight . . .
> Yet if you're bent upon it, while you dine,
> Some interval to that grand work assign. . . .

> If you your knife not over-keen survey,
> Fraught with the pudding of a former day,
> These ills are soon remov'd – put off your shoe
> Which for a whetstone very well may do:
> Then on the sole, by frequent rubs subdu'd,
> Its rust shall vanish, and its edge be good. . . .

> Do lumps of meat between thy teeth inhere?
> Remove them soon, my worthy pioneer!
> The crocodile, tho' famed for wily tricks,
> When to his jaws large bits of food affix,
> Finds to his cost the grievance can't be stirr'd,
> But by the assistance of a silly bird;
> He gapes: the win'g inhabitant of air
> Does to his mouth, in hopes of prey, repair,
> In ev'ry hollow tooth securely peak,
> And pick from thence th' incumbrance with his beak.
> From you to art be small assistance ow'd,
> Fingers and hands hath Nature's self bestow'd;
> Then or your fingers or your knife apply,
> Nor on the assistance of a bird rely.

Finally, to reveal the true manners of the upper classes in the age of elegance, here are some extracts from Richard Graves's introduction to his translation of the *Galateo*, published in 1774:

I remember a country gentleman, not long since, who could write himself Armigero . . . that at a public ordinary, borrowed a tooth-pick of a stranger, who sat next him; and having made use of it, wiped it clean, and (without the least sense of anything indelicate in the affair) thankfully returned it to the owner. . . .

I also heard the mayor of a respectable borough hem and expectorate in so vociferous a manner, as not only to startle the company, but to alarm the whole neighbourhood, and then compose himself in his elbow-chair, with the utmost complacency and satisfaction, as felicitating himself upon his having been able to perform his animal functions with so much vigour and elasticity. . . .

Belinda, after dinner, rummages the most remote cavities of her mouth and gums, with the corner of her napkin; and then squirts out the soiled ablution into the water-glass, with so bold and ostentatious an air, as if she considered it as an excellence, and an infallible mark of her familiarity with the bon ton of fashionable life.

Clelia spits in her handkerchief with so little sense of indelicacy, that, instead of any endeavours to conceal it, she displays it with an ambitious air before the company. . . .

I knew a very ingenious physician, and a very worthy man, who was dismissed from his attendance on a noble family, for no other reason, than for a habit he had got of spitting upon the carpet.

Behaviour of this sort would have been unthinkable in the best nineteenth-century circles, at any rate after Victoria had come to the throne and the gospel of good form had been established. To explain how the great change came about, it is not sufficient to point simply to the development of industry, as though Victorianism were merely an economic phenomenon resulting from increased wealth. Economic conditions by themselves could not have accounted for so great a change in manners, but they could, and did, bring greatly increased influence to a class whose attitude to life was very different from that of the old aristocracy. The Victorian outlook was essentially middle class and its origins went back considerably further than the industrial revolution. It was largely the middle classes who had tackled the problem of social reform during the two preceding centuries, and in order to understand the manners of the nineteenth century it is necessary first of all to consider briefly the nature of their long crusade against vice.

It is unlikely that the gentlemen's books of the sixteenth and seventeenth centuries were of much benefit to the unlettered poor, who could do little more than ape the behaviour of those who were better provided than themselves. In the early Stuart period expanding trade swelled the pockets of the gentry and the squires, while many of the poorer class were only saved by the poor law from the worst excesses of poverty, especially in London, which was growing fast, and in the other cities. These were not the conditions in which a proper regard for nice manners was likely to prevail. Into this world of poverty came the Puritans, who did what they could to abolish sport, gaming, and drink, and by spreading the delusion that what is nice is *de facto* naughty were responsible for making the poor man's life even more miserable than it need have been. The result was not what they had hoped but exactly the opposite. With no effective police force to keep order, robbery, brawling, and prostitution enormously increased. By the end of the century the situation had become serious enough to alarm the more sober-minded, and in 1692 a 'Society for the Reformation of Manners' was instituted with the object of teaching the poor how they should behave. 'Manners', in the language of the Society, meant such virtues as temperance, prudence, and thrift, for what we nowadays understand by the word was in those days commonly known as 'civility' and social polish of this sort was hardly to be expected in the poor.

In 1694 the Society issued a volume containing its *Proposals for a National Reformation of Manners*. They asked, among other things, that there should be a general fast, by way of doing penance; that care should be taken 'to establish justice and judgement unto the poor and the needy'; that play-houses should be suppressed; and that 'great care be taken to put a difference between the clean and the unclean members (the vile and the honourable) in the visible Church'. These proposals were followed by a list of the prostitutes who had been fined or whipped during the previous year, a clear indication of how the Society intended to set about its task of reform. It was obvious that while they aimed to use drastic measures to suppress the vices of the poor, they were prepared to turn a blind eye upon lack of virtue in the rich. Defoe was quick to seize upon this hypocritical method of purification. In *The Poor Man's Plea* (1698) he suggested that reform should begin with the well-to-do, and in 1702 he followed up the attack with a poem called 'Reformation of Manners: a Satyr'. In spite of this the Society continued to fasten its attention upon the degraded habits of the poor. Cheap gin was an added obstacle to its efforts in the first half of the eighteenth century, but the reformers eventually found an ally in tea, which became more plentiful in the second.

In the meantime the established clergy sided with the unassailable rich and tended to retire into the peace of their vicarages, leaving gospelling to the dissenters, whose following was largely among the less well-off. The Society for the Promotion of Christian Knowledge, a Church of England body founded in 1698, did what it could to help in the crusade by distributing tracts, but in general such efforts were poorly supported by the clergy, who, in country parishes at least, like Chaucer's monk, often gave more of their time to the hunting of the fox than to the cure of souls. This was not entirely their own fault, for much of the blame must be laid at the door of a system by which benefices depended upon the goodwill of rich patrons. The congregations, too, were likely to find harsh sermons tiresome, for they were not unduly devout. A passage in *The Man of Manners*, which has already been mentioned, sums up the attitude both of pulpit and of pew.

A truly polite divine, who means to rise in the world, and not always continue a rush-light in the Church, must prudently avoid such doctrines, as may make people of quality's seats uneasy to them; he must not preach up vertue, not only as an ornament to them, but a strict obligation; for this would be to lampoon and expose his betters. 'Tis true, he may have Scripture for his warrant; but still it would be flying in the face of great people, and be deem'd an unpardonable piece of rudeness and ill manners. . . .

Ogling fans, as well as novels, plays, and poems, bound and gilt in the form and manner of Common-Prayer-Books, the use of them, in any church, or chapel in England, and Wales, and town of Berwick upon Tweed, I think ought to be restrained under severe penalties.

Towards the end of the century an attempt was made to make up leeway by the opening of the first Sunday schools. The most forceful personality behind the new movement was Hannah More, who, in a different vein, took up the cudgels relinquished by Defoe when she published, in 1788, a book called *Thoughts on the Importance of the Manners of the Great to General Society*. She thought of the Sunday schools more as a means of curbing delinquency than as missions of salvation, but it is nevertheless true that the ceaseless preaching of reform, aided by the spectre of revolution across the Channel, had at last begun to make some headway among the wealthier classes. The middle classes were, in principle, converted already, since they had been the most receptive to the Methodist appeal. As a result the strength of the Church of England began to revive and numerous pious societies were formed for the purpose of giving comfort, both spiritual and material, to the poor. It would be uncharitable to question their motives and certainly wrong to assume that they were not sincerely religious, but to some at least the movement must have had extra appeal as a form of insurance against social upheaval.

Meanwhile the industrial revolution was swelling the ranks of the middle class, which, in a generation or two, was to take over the leadership of society from the old aristocracy. Its novitiate was to be the public school, and Victoria and Albert were to be its patron saints. At the turn of the century it was possible to make out what lay ahead. The name of Mrs Grundy[1] was first bandied across the footlights in 1798 and it was not long after this that Thomas Bowdler, the expurgator, began his task of chastening English literature for polite ears. His public was assured, for many readers felt that indelicacy and profanity were as much out of place in literature as they were in polite conversation. A letter in the *Gentleman's Magazine* for December 1791 had already shown which way the wind was blowing.

It is well known that, for some time past, neither man, woman nor child, in Great Britain or Ireland, of any rank or fashion, has been subject to that gross kind of exsudation which was formerly known by the name of sweat; and that now every mortal, except carters, coal-heavers, and Irish chairmen (animals all *sui generis*, and therefore not included within the general description of other British subjects), merely perspires. . . .

All our mothers and grand-mothers used in due course of time to become with-child . . . but it is very well known, that no female, above the degree of a chambermaid or laundress, has been with child these ten years past: every decent married woman now becomes pregnant.

1. Mrs Grundy was created by Thomas Morton in his comedy *Speed the Plough*, which was first performed in London in 1798. She does not herself appear in the play, but is continually mentioned by one of the chief characters, Dame Ashfield, who is perpetually worried about what Mrs Grundy will think or say of her conduct. She has thus become the symbol of respectability and propriety.

Such prudery was new, and with it came a new sense of righteousness. Public opinion was becoming sufficiently sensitive to scandal to drive Byron out of the country and to make a martyr of Queen Caroline, if only because her indiscretions were unproven while those of her husband were flagrant.

The French Revolution was a powerful ally on the side of reform, for while it corrupted continental manners, it caused English manners to stiffen in reaction. John Eustace, writing in 1813, pointed out that London had now taken the place of Paris and Turin in leadership of the polite world.

The court of Versailles was formerly considered the most polished court in the world, and the state of society in the higher classes at Paris, as well as at Rome and Turin, was supposed to have reached a very high degree of refinement. The principal object of travelling then was to acquire, in such accomplished society, that ease and those graces which constitute the perfection of good breeding, and were seldom, it was then fancied, to be discovered in the manners of a home-bred Englishman. . . . But the case is very different at present. The French Revolution has been as fatal to the manners as to the morals of nations; it has corrupted the one and brutalized the other. . . . London, that has long been the first city in Europe for population, extent, and opulence is now also confessedly the first in point of society, and the capital of the polite and fashionable, as it has long been of the commercial world.

It was, therefore, in the capital of the polite and fashionable world that Victoria mounted the throne and succeeded her less respectable uncles, amid the plaudits of all the Mrs Grundys of England. The long campaign to achieve respectability at last had a royal patron. Contact with foreign society, now much easier, helped to strengthen the conviction that the British, in addition to the material advantages with which they were blessed, were also racially and morally superior to the rest of the world. It was this belief that determined their manners, for whatever may have been the true state of their morals – and they were certainly much better than those of their grandfathers – the Victorians were determined that their outward behaviour at least should do full justice to the fine conception they had of themselves and their mission. If they were to succeed, they had to insist on the very strictest standards of formal etiquette, and a society such as theirs provided a very good market for instructional books containing the rules of good form, like the ritual of a new religion. So many were published that it would be quite impossible to deal with even a fraction of them here. They ranged from pocket-sized manuals to exhaustive works which explained all the complications of social life. You could learn from them, for instance, the order of precedence for going in to dinner. If you were a barrister's wife you could expect to be led in ahead of a doctor's or officer's consort, and so on. You could also learn the etiquette of visiting cards and the right method of introducing strangers, how many days you should allow to elapse before writing a bread and butter letter, and the proper procedure at dances, picnics, and tea parties. Young ladies were instructed that not all their partners at dances were alike desirable acquaintances and an introduction at a dance by night was not sufficient ground for recognizing the same young man in the street the next morning. Good form would require that a real gentleman should get himself properly introduced later on. There were also chapters on correct dress, warnings against ostentatious jewelry and strong perfumes, and hints on personal cleanliness, bathing, and the care of the nails and teeth.

It is impossible to give an adequate selection from nineteenth-century books of manners, but perhaps some short extracts from one of them can be taken as typical. One of the most authoritative of Victorian writers on all sorts of useful knowledge was Samuel Beeton, husband of the famous Isabella, who is still regarded as an oracle on household management, though with increasing consternation. In 1876 his name was used to give publicity to a book entitled *Manners of Polite Society*, though it is doubtful whether he had a hand in composing it. It was a combined edition of three shorter works originally addressed to gentlemen, ladies, and the family respectively.

## Etiquette for Gentlemen

Never wear, if possible, a coloured shirt. Figures and stripes do not conceal impurity, nor should this be a desideratum with any decent man. . . .

Wadding or stuffing should be avoided as much as possible. A little may be judiciously used to round off the more salient points of an angular figure, but when it is used for the purpose of creating an egregiously false impression of superior form, it is simply snobbish. . . .

Soup will constitute the first course, which must be noiselessly supped from the side of a spoon. It is impolite to ask for a second plate. . . .

Your knife should never be put in your mouth. The four- or five-pronged fork, now in general use, is for this purpose. If you cannot manage with a fork, try a spoon. . . .

The waltz, or 'valse', as it is now called, is a very old favourite, and, in the form of the valse à deux temps, occupies a conspicuous place in the ball-room programme. Those who believe that a lady should never come into near personal contact with any gentleman not a near relation, or a probable or actual husband, must still object to this and all similar dances, for in no other are two persons brought so near to each other, and none exercises so great an influence over the senses and emotions. Doubtless it should be engaged in with caution by all sensitive organizations. . . .

If a lady waltz with you, beware not to press her waist; you must only lightly touch it with the palm of your hand, lest you leave a disagreeable impression, not only on her ceinture, but on her mind. . . .

No one can safely resort to the bath when the bodily powers are much weakened, by whatever cause; and though it is unwise to use it directly after taking a full meal, it should not immediately precede the chief meal of the day, if that be taken at a late hour, and after prolonged abstinence and exertion. . . .

If you use tobacco, never omit to rinse the mouth thoroughly after smoking, and never substitute a strong odour for water, especially when going into the society of ladies. . . .

It is said that bathing the backs of the ears with cold water contributes to preserve the teeth. . . .

Bathing forms a natural and most important auxiliary of the toilette; it is an agreeable as well as healthful practice, and was in general use and esteem among the early civilized nations of the world, but has fallen into comparative neglect with us, except as a kind of compulsory measure toward the restoration of health . . .

*Etiquette for Ladies*

When a stranger offers to assist you over a puddle, or something of the kind, do not hesitate or decline, as if you thought he was taking an unwarrantable liberty. . . .

Rocking chairs are now seldom seen in a parlour; handsome, stuffed easy chairs that are moved on castors are substituted. . . .

The fashion of wearing black silk mittens at breakfast is now obsolete. It was always inconvenient, and neither useful nor ornamental. . . .

It is an insult to the company, and a disgrace to yourself to dip into a dish anything that has been, even for a moment, in your mouth. To take butter or salt with your own knife is an abomination. It is nearly as bad to take a lump of sugar with your fingers. . . .

No lady looks worse than when gnawing a bone, even of game or poultry. Few ladies do it. In fact, nothing should be sucked or gnawed in public. Always pare apples and peaches, and crack no nuts with the teeth. . . .

*Family etiquette*

Metal toothpicks have a pernicious effect on the teeth, and those made from quills irritate the gum; indeed, the only safe article to use is a piece of cane or slip of light wood cut to a nice point. . . .

Purity of breath is an unspeakable personal comfort, and its value in social intercourse is literally beyond that of rubies. . . .

The following are things not to be done: Biting your nails. . . . Sitting cross-kneed and jogging your feet. . . . Humming a tune before strangers. Singing as you go up and downstairs. Putting your arm around the neck of another young girl, or promenading the room with arms encircling waists. . . . Slapping a gentleman with your handkerchief or tapping him with your fan.

Nowadays etiquette is less rigid than it was before the First World War, but this does not necessarily mean that manners are worse. It is important to distinguish between the two, because this is the difference between books like the *Galateo*, which deal with the principles of good manners, and the majority of the Victorian manuals, which gave most of their space to details of etiquette.